Finger Food

Finger Food

Text by Norman Kolpas

CollinsPublishersSanFrancisco

A Division of HarperCollins*Publishers*

First published in USA 1996 by Collins Publishers San Francisco
1160 Battery Street, San Francisco, CA 94111-1213
HarperCollins Web Site: http://www.harpercollins.com

Produced by Weldon Owen Inc.

Associate Publisher: Anne Dickerson
Managing Editor: Judith Dunham
Editorial Assistant: Hannah Rahill
Text Author: Norman Kolpas
Copy Editor: Judith Dunham
Proofreaders: Ken DellaPenta and Sharilyn Hovind
Index: Ken DellaPenta
Design Concept: John Bull
Design: Kari Perin, Perin + Perin
Collins Publishers San Francisco
Series Editor: Meesha Halm
Production: Lynne Noone, Susan Swant, Kristen Wurz

Library of Congress Cataloging-in-Publication Data
Kolpas, Norman.
Finger food / text by Norman Kolpas.
p.   cm. — (Easy entertaining series)
At head of title: Featuring recipes from the best-selling Beautiful Cookbook series.
Includes index.
ISBN 0-00-225048-9
1. Appetizers. 2. Entertaining. 3. Cookery.
I. Title. II. Series.
TX740.K659   1996
641.8' 12—dc20   95-50522

Manufactured by Toppan
Printed in China
1 3 5 7 9 10 8 6 4 2

*Front cover, top to bottom: Crab-Stuffed Mushrooms (recipe page 29),
Wild Mushroom Filo Packets (recipe page 31)
Page 2, outside to center: Spinach Pancakes with Sour Cream and Salmon Roe
(recipe page 49), Smoked Salmon Lavash Rolls (recipe page 37)*

CONTENTS

Introduction   7

The Well-Stocked Pantry   9

The Art of Presentation   18

Menus   20

Wrapped, Rolled & Stuffed   25

Nachos & Canapés   47

From Brochettes to Nuts   71

Index   95

INTRODUCTION

Food, one of life's great pleasures, becomes more pleasurable still when eaten with the fingers. Adding the sense of touch to those senses that come into play when we eat—sight, smell and taste—heightens the experience. At the same time, touch delightfully reminds us of childhood, those carefree days before we mastered the use of utensils.

No wonder finger food is perfect to serve when you entertain. When you set out platters and bowls filled with tempting morsels for guests to pop into their mouths by hand, you've instantly set an incomparably relaxed tone.

The occasion may be as casual as an afternoon gathering around the television or as formal as black-tie cocktails at sunset. Easy-to-make finger food can always be found to match the style of your party. They can also be counted on to satisfy your guests as they stimulate conversation: "Ooh, what are those?" "I'm not sure, but they're delicious!"

This book aims to excite just such conversations at your own parties by offering, in a concise, convenient format, a wealth of information, inspiration and kitchen-tested recipes for fabulous finger food from around the world. On the following pages, you'll find tips and hints for planning, shopping for, preparing and serving finger food when you entertain. This introductory section concludes with suggested menus for eight different kinds of parties featuring finger food—clearly showing that a selection of these easy-to-serve-and-eat appetizers alone can make up a well-rounded, satisfying meal.

The forty-four recipes that make up the heart of this book are divided into three chapters to help you plan a menu of dishes that are varied in their form as well as their ingredients. In the first, you'll find finger food that is wrapped, rolled or stuffed, from Greek dolmas to Asian spring rolls, from Russian piroshki to Mexican chilies rellenos. The next chapter features finger-food sandwiches in a variety so vast that it embraces the cheese-topped Mexican appetizers known as nachos and *pissaladière*, French cousin to the pizza. Finally, you'll encounter a chapter that proves how diverse finger food can really be, including as it does onion rings to olives, chilled prawns to hot-off-the-grill kebabs of pork and chicken.

Special features built into the recipes make this book more useful still. Those with the 🌱 symbol next to their titles are vegetarian. Most recipes suggest ingredient substitutions or variations that let you adapt them to your or your guests' tastes or dietary needs. These options also encourage you to be creative as you cook the recipes again and again.

What all these dishes have in common is their utter convenience, in both their preparation and their consumption. As you leaf through the recipes, you'll note that they may be made well in advance of your party or that they are a cinch to whip up at almost a moment's notice. Convenience foods—such as frozen pastry and filo doughs and canned chicken stock—make the work easier and quicker still.

The range of recipes promotes creativity in your entertaining. As the menus only begin to suggest, there are enough choices to allow you to compose a menu based on a seasonal theme, a special occasion or a kind of food that you or guests might particularly enjoy. A menu can give rise to ideas for decorative themes and other ways to set the mood, which you'll find discussed on pages 18–19.

This book frees you to pay attention to the other details of your party. With finger food, easy entertaining can be—quite literally—at your fingertips.

THE WELL-STOCKED PANTRY

Whether you boast a walk-in pantry that recalls the grand houses of times past, or a modest one that occupies a portion of your kitchen cupboard, that food storage space can form the foundation for easy entertaining with finger foods. Scanning the recipe ingredients lists in this book, you'll see common items that can readily be stored and for fairly long time periods. These will make up the backbone of your pantry and, once stocked, promise only brief shopping trips for any fresh foods you need to complete your party menu.

OILS

Oils of all kinds serve a number of key purposes in the preparation of finger foods. Fried foods generally rely on flavorless vegetable and seed oils such as those from corn, safflower seeds and peanuts. These oils can achieve, without smoking, the high temperatures necessary for deep-frying, and they allow the natural taste of foods to come through, imparting none of their own flavor.

When an oil's flavor is desired, particularly in marinades, dressings and sauces, the oil of choice is often olive oil. Seek out the best-quality olive oil you can find. Products labeled "extra-virgin" are the finest, distinguished by their fruity aroma, full-bodied flavor and clear, deep green color—all resulting from the fact that they are processed on the first pressing of the olives, without the use of heat or chemicals. They are also notable for having the lowest acid content among grades of olive oil. Grades labeled "virgin" or "pure" have somewhat higher acidity and less flavor, and are better suited to cooking.

Storage: Store all oils in airtight containers in a cool, dark place, using them within 6 months of the date of purchase. Do not purchase oils in larger quantities than you are likely to use in that time period.

VINEGARS

Whether used as part of a dressing, a dip or a marinade, good vinegar lends spark to many finger foods with its sharp acidity and the particular character of the wine or spirit from which it is derived. A well-stocked pantry should include good-quality vinegars made from both red and white wines, as well as an assortment of others such as sherry vinegar, malt vinegar and Japanese rice vinegar. Many cooks today consider balsamic vinegar a necessity. Made in Modena, Italy, from reduced grape juice aged for years in a succession of ever-smaller wooden casks, it has a deep reddish brown color and a distinctively rich, sweet-sour flavor.

Storage: Keep vinegars up to 6 months stored in airtight containers in a cool, dark place.

STOCKS

Essences of poultry, meat, seafood or vegetables that have been slowly simmered with aromatic herbs and other seasonings to extract their flavor, stocks are essential cooking liquids and moistening and flavoring agents for a wide variety of savory dishes. Most home cooks today haven't the time to make their own stock, so your pantry should include cans of good-quality stock, usually labeled "broth." Seek those without salt or with reduced salt. They allow you greater leeway in seasoning to taste the recipes in which they are used. Also look for some of the excellent frozen stocks carried in the frozen food sections of some markets.

Storage: Though canned stocks will keep indefinitely in the pantry, you should nonetheless aim to use them within 1 year. Keep frozen stocks in the coldest part of your freezer and use within 3 months.

OLIVES, CAPERS AND ANCHOVIES

These three Mediterranean specialties, all of which are prized for the sharp taste that results from preservation by salting, have found their way into finger foods worldwide. Keeping a supply on hand ensures that you can readily add their distinctive spark to party dishes.

Olives are a quintessential finger food. Both green (unripe) and black (ripe) varieties are cured in salt, brine, vinegar or oil, with a wide range of seasonings, to yield flavors from mild and mellow to pungent and spicy. Green olives are also sold pitted and stuffed with pimiento, anchovies, capers, garlic or almonds. French Niçoise and Greek Kalamata olives—both of which are brine-cured black varieties—are familiar staples, sold in good-quality delicatessens. Look, too, for Italian salt-cured Gaeta olives.

Capers, the small, round buds of a bush native to the Mediterranean, range from the size of a peppercorn to that of a pea. They may be pickled in vinegar or packed in salt; the latter require light rinsing before use. For the finest flavor, seek out imported capers.

Anchovies, distinctively savory and salty, may be used whole, chopped or finely mashed, either to impart a subtle flavor or to give a distinctive character to appetizers. They are commonly sold as fillets, packed flat in oil in cans; those packed in olive oil are preferable. Whole, salt-preserved anchovies may also sometimes be found, packed in large cans or sold by the pound, in some delicatessens. They require filleting and light rinsing before use.

Storage: Keep unopened canned or bottled olives in a cool, dark place for up to 6 months; once opened, they should be transferred to a nonmetallic container and refrigerated for 2–3 weeks. Bottled capers can be stored for several months in the refrigerator, salted capers for several months at cool room temperature. Canned anchovies, unopened, can be stored for 1 year at cool room temperature. Once opened, they can be refrigerated for 1–2 days.

HERBS AND SPICES

The kitchen pantry extends easily into a windowsill, balcony, patio or garden when you grow your own fresh herbs—such as dill, parsley, oregano, chives, thyme, lemon thyme, cilantro and tarragon—for use as seasonings or garnishes. If time or inclination prevents you from doing this, look for fresh herbs in the vegetable section of a well-stocked supermarket.

Seek out dried herbs and spices—including black and white peppercorns, nutmeg, paprika, red pepper flakes, cumin, cayenne pepper and the other herbs and spices used in the recipes in this book—in the seasonings section of a well-stocked supermarket. Try to buy them from a market with a regular turnover of products, which ensures the most recently dried, fullest flavored seasonings.

Storage: Keep fresh herbs wrapped in a damp paper towel in the refrigerator, where they will last for up to 1 week. Mark dried herbs and spices with their date of purchase, and store in airtight containers in a cool, dry place. Use or replace them within 1 year.

BREADS, CRACKERS AND PASTRIES

Cut into slices or pulled apart into hunks, any bread becomes finger food. Buy yours from a local market that carries a good selection of freshly baked, unsliced loaves, or seek out one of the small boutique bakeries that are popping up with increasing frequency. Crackers of all kinds, whether graced with a topping or unadorned, also make one of the most convenient, versatile and appealing of ready-made appetizers. Offer your guests at least two or three different choices. Well-stocked supermarkets and specialty-food stores offer a good supply.

Most markets today also carry in their freezer cases frozen puff pastry, shortcrust pastry and bread doughs, ready to wrap around fillings or shape into miniature pizzas.

Storage: Keep fresh bread in a plastic bag in a cool, dark place, where it should remain in good condition for 1–2 days. Store crackers in an airtight container in a cool, dark place and use within 3 months. Keep frozen doughs in the coldest part of the freezer and use within 2–3 months.

CHEESE

As well as topping or forming part of the filling for an infinite number of finger foods, cheese reigns in its own right as one of the most popular appetizers imaginable. Cut it into cubes or sticks, spread it on crackers or bread, or simply set out large blocks of cheese with knives or shavers, and guests feel as if they've been treated to a feast.

Whatever the kind of finger food party you plan to offer, cheese makes an excellent, easy addition to the menu. When serving more than one type of cheese, aim for a good variety that provides something for every taste: well-aged Cheddar; mild Monterey Jack; nutty Swiss; well-ripened Brie or Camembert; sharp, crumbly Parmesan; rich, tangy goat cheese; creamy blue cheese.

Storage: Refrigerate cheeses, well wrapped to prevent them from drying out, for 1–2 weeks. Let them come to room temperature for about 1 hour before serving.

VEGETABLES AND FRUITS

Virtually the entire produce section of the local market is at your disposal for use as finger foods: sticks of crisp carrots, celery or jícama; whole button mushrooms, radishes or cherry tomatoes; lightly blanched florets of broccoli or cauliflower; whole snow peas or sugar snap peas; seedless grapes; pear slices; navel orange segments; fresh, plump summer figs; tangerines, ready to peel and eat.

Let whatever is freshest, highest in quality and lowest in price at your local market dictate your choices when you entertain. Don't ignore fruits and vegetables as possible centerpieces, too, whether you display a bowl of gleaming autumn apples, an assortment of colorful bell peppers or squashes, a luscious cluster of grapes or a gaily colored ornamental cabbage.

Storage: Fresh vegetables such as greens or mushrooms should be used within 2–3 days of purchase. Store hardier vegetables such as carrots, celery, radishes and zucchini in the refrigerator for up to 1 week. Store most ripe fruits in the refrigerator—citrus fruits for 3–4 weeks, others for about 1 week—and let them come to room temperature before serving.

SPECIALTY INGREDIENTS

The following international foods from the recipes in this book can be found in well-stocked supermarkets or can be purchased from ethnic or specialty-food markets.

ASIAN FOODS

Bean sprouts: The fresh, crunchy sprouts of the mung bean are available in most markets. If unavailable, substitute canned bean sprouts.

Chinese sausage: Sweet, rich and flavorful, these dried, slender pork sausages, each about 6 inches in length, are usually sold strung in pairs. They keep in the refrigerator for several weeks or can be frozen for several months if wrapped airtight.

Coconut milk: Found canned or bottled, this liquid extract of grated coconut flesh adds richness and subtle sweetness to recipes. The thick top layer that forms when the milk settles is sometimes called coconut cream, or simply thick coconut milk, and may be sold separately.

Daikon: This long, sausage-shaped Japanese white radish has a mild, slightly bitter and peppery flavor and a refreshingly crisp texture. Daikon is eaten raw as a garnish. It is also grated as a seasoning.

Fish sauce: The liquid collected from small fish or shrimp that are salted and fermented in jars, this salty, pale brown sauce seasons many Southeast Asian dishes.

Garlic and chili sauce: This commercial condiment or seasoning made of red chilies, garlic, vinegar and salt is usually sold in large squeeze bottles.

Pickled ginger slices: Thinly sliced fresh ginger pickled in rice vinegar is used as a garnish in Japanese cooking.

Rice vinegar: Japanese vinegar made from rice wine is sold either mild and plain or seasoned.

Sesame seeds: With their rich, nutlike flavor, these small, teardrop-shaped ivory or black seeds are a popular garnish in Japanese, Chinese and other Asian cuisines.

Soy sauce: Enjoyed throughout Asia, this kitchen and table seasoning is made from soybeans, wheat, salt and water. Chinese soy sauces tend to be saltier than those from Japan. Products labeled "dark" have a richer flavor. Sweetened, spiced soy sauces are also popular in Indonesian and Southeast Asian cuisines. Buy good-quality, imported products.

Spring roll wrappers: These thin, shiny Chinese noodle squares, measuring 7–8 inches on a side, are used to wrap spring rolls. Do not confuse them with thicker, fresh egg roll wrappers. Sold fresh or frozen, they may be stored for 1 week in the refrigerator or up to 2 months wrapped airtight in the freezer.

Thai rice papers: Thin, dried noodle sheets made from ground rice flour, these papers are softened with water and used as wrappers for fresh spring rolls.

Tofu: Made from a milky extract of fresh soybeans, this custardlike curd is popular throughout Asia.

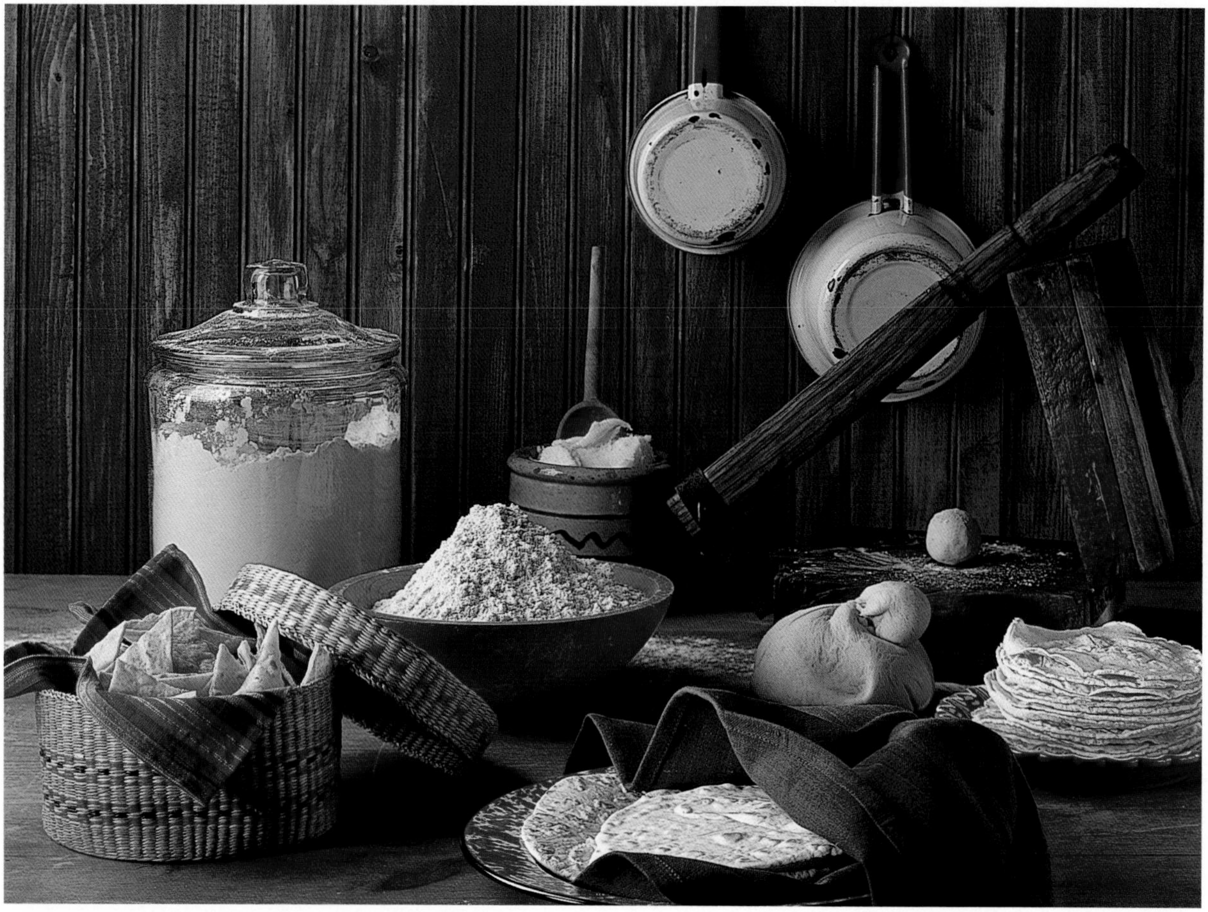

LATIN AMERICAN FOODS

Chilies: These staples of Mexican and American Southwestern cooking come fresh and dried in a wide range of colors, shapes, sizes, flavors and degrees of heat. Fresh chilies include the Anaheim, jalapeño, poblano, serrano and habanero; dried, the ancho, chipotle and pasilla. Preserved chilies are available both canned and bottled. When using any hot chili, it's a good idea to add only a portion of the amount called for, then taste for heat before adding more. See page 16 for a precautionary note on the preparation of chilies.

Cotija cheese: Similar in taste and texture to Parmesan, this hard, dry, aged full-flavored cheese is crumbled as a garnish or as part of a filling.

Jícama: Also known as the yam bean or Mexican potato, this knobbly root vegetable has a thick, fibrous brown skin that conceals crisp, white flesh possessing a slightly sweet flavor and crunchy texture. It is usually eaten raw, cut into sticks as finger food. It will keep for weeks, unpeeled, in the refrigerator.

Pumpkin seeds: Also known by the Mexican name *pepitas,* these hulled, dark green seeds can be toasted and salted as a finger food or added to savory or sweet dishes.

Queso Fresco: This fresh Mexican-style cheese made from Grade A milk has the texture of farmer's cheese and the taste of Monterey Jack. It is crumbled and used as a garnish or in finger-food fillings.

Tortillas: Thin, circular and unleavened, tortillas are made from dough of ground corn, and less frequently wheat, quickly cooked on a griddle. The bread of Mexico, they can serve as edible wrappers for finger foods. Cut into wedges and fried until crisp (page 16), they are also used as the bases for nachos and other canapés.

MEDITERRANEAN & MIDDLE EASTERN FOODS

Feta cheese: Made from sheep's or goat's milk, this white, crumbly cheese—a specialty of Greece and Turkey—has a sharp, salty flavor and a consistency that ranges from creamy to dry.

Filo dough: Taking its name from the Greek word for "leaf," this flour and water pastry consists of fragile, tissue-thin sheets that are used to form crisp wrappers for both savory and sweet finger foods. Filo is commonly sold frozen; defrost before use. Handle filo carefully to avoid tearing, and keep unused sheets moist by covering them with a slightly damp, clean towel.

Goat cheese: Prized for its fresh, creamy taste and texture and its sharp tang, goat cheese is sometimes called by its French name, *chèvre.* Goat cheese is sold in cylinders, rounds and other shapes and may be coated with ground pepper or herbs.

Grape leaves: Used as edible wrappers for Greek and other Middle Eastern finger foods, bottled grape leaves packed in brine should be rinsed gently to remove their brine.

Lavash: This crisp, flat cracker bread is usually sold in large rounds. The rounds can be broken into pieces and used as bases for hors d'oeuvres. Softened lavash can be wrapped around various fillings and sliced into finger food.

Pita bread: These round or oval, flat pocket breads—also known by the Turkish name *pide*—are frequently cut into wedges and crisped on a grill or under a broiler for use as a base for finger foods.

PANTRY TECHNIQUES

The following basic techniques are called for in the recipes in this book or offer alternatives to store-bought ingredients. Prepare and store them as you wish to add to your home pantry.

CLARIFYING BUTTER

Place 1 cup unsalted butter in a small saucepan and melt over low heat without stirring. With a spoon, skim off and discard any white foam from the surface of the melted butter. Then slowly and gently pour the clear liquid butter into a container, stopping before any of the milky residue below it leaves the pan; discard the residue. Clarified butter will keep 3–4 weeks in an airtight container in the refrigerator and may be frozen for several weeks longer.

FRYING TOFU

Drain the tofu well in a colander, then cut into $1/2$-inch squares. In a deep, heavy frying pan over medium-high heat, pour vegetable oil to a depth of 1 inch. Add the tofu squares and fry until golden brown on all sides, 2–3 minutes. Using a slotted spoon or wire skimmer, transfer the cubes to paper towels to drain. The fried tofu can be stored in an airtight container in the refrigerator for 1–2 days.

GRATING AND CUTTING CITRUS ZEST

To grate the thin outermost layer of colorful, aromatic and flavorful zest from a citrus fruit's skin, rub the fruit against the fine rasps of a handheld grater. You can also draw the sharp, small cutting holes of a special zesting tool along the skin to remove the zest in very fine strips. For larger strips of zest, draw a swivel-bladed vegetable peeler along the fruit's skin, then cut or chop the resulting strips to the desired size or consistency. Whatever method you use, take care not to remove any of the bitter white pith beneath the zest.

HANDLING CHILIES

Chilies contain capsaicin, which can irritate the skin or eyes and must be handled with care. About 90 percent of this substance is found in a chili's ribs and seeds. When working with chilies, wear rubber gloves and do not rub your eyes or face. As soon as the work is done, thoroughly wash your hands and any utensils you have used with warm soapy water.

MAKING BREAD CRUMBS

Using a less than fresh but still flavorful loaf, first cut it into slices and, if desired, trim off the crusts. Process in a food processor fitted with the metal blade or in a blender, or place on a cutting surface and flake into crumbs with a fork. For dried crumbs, arrange the fresh crumbs in an even, thin layer on a baking sheet and bake in a preheated 325°F oven until thoroughly dried, 15–20 minutes. One slice of bread yields about $3/4$ cup fresh or $1/4$ cup dried crumbs. Store any leftovers in an airtight, heavy-duty plastic bag in the freezer for up to 3 months.

MAKING TORTILLA CHIPS

When preparing nachos or any other finger foods that use corn tortilla chips as a base, you'll achieve a fresher taste—and greater control over salt and other seasonings—if you make your own chips. Cut corn tortillas into 6 wedges each. In a deep, heavy frying pan, heat $1 1/2$–2 inches of corn or vegetable oil to 360°F on a deep-frying thermometer, or until a small piece of tortilla starts to brown within moments of being

dropped in the oil. Working in batches to avoid overcrowding the pan, add the tortilla wedges and fry until crisp and golden, 30–60 seconds. Using a slotted spoon or wire skimmer, transfer the chips to paper towels to drain. Sprinkle with salt, if desired. The chips will keep for 2–3 days stored in an airtight container at room temperature.

PEELING AND DEVEINING SHRIMP

Fresh shrimp are usually peeled before cooking, and their thin, dark, veinlike intestinal tracts removed. Insert your thumbs between the two rows of legs and peel away the shell by pulling it apart. Discard the shell. Using a small, sharp knife, make a slit along the back of the shrimp to reveal the vein, and pull it out with the knife tip or your fingers.

PEELING AND SEEDING TOMATOES

To peel a fresh tomato, first bring a saucepan of water to a boil and fill a mixing bowl with cold water. With a small, sharp knife, cut a shallow X in the tomato's blossom end. Immerse the tomato in the boiling water for about 15 seconds, then plunge it into the bowl of cold water. Cut out the stem end and, with your fingers or a knife, pull off the skin. To seed the tomato, cut it in half and gently squeeze out the seeds, or scoop them out with your fingers or a small knife. Peeled tomatoes may be stored in an airtight container in the refrigerator for 3–4 days.

PITTING OLIVES

A special olive-pitting tool allows you simultaneously to grip the olive and to push out the pit with one squeeze of your hand. Alternatively, you can use a small, sharp knife to slit the olive lengthwise down to its pit, prying or carefully cutting the pit away from the flesh.

ROASTING BELL PEPPERS AND CHILIES

Many recipes call for bell peppers and chilies to be roasted in order to remove their tough, indigestible skins and to heighten their flavor and texture. Arrange the peppers or chilies on a baking sheet and place under a preheated broiler; set them directly on a grill rack over a charcoal fire; or spear them, one at a time, on a fork and hold over an open flame. Turn as needed until the skins are evenly blackened and blistered on all sides. Remove from the heat and cover with a kitchen towel or place in a paper bag until cool enough to handle, about 10 minutes. With your fingers or a small knife, peel off the blackened skins. Then remove the stems and seeds and cut or tear as directed in individual recipes. Peeled, roasted peppers can be stored in an airtight container in the refrigerator for up to 3 days.

ROASTING GARLIC

When roasted, garlic loses its sharp edge and develops a mellow flavor and soft, smooth consistency. To roast a whole head of garlic, cut a shallow incision around its circumference with a small, sharp knife, taking care to pierce the skin without cutting through the cloves. Peel off the outer papery skin from the top half of the head. Place the garlic in a baking dish, sprinkle with salt and pepper and drizzle with about $1/4$ cup of olive oil. Bake in a preheated 225°F oven for about 20 minutes; then cover with foil and bake until very soft, basting occasionally with the oil in the dish.

The Art of Presentation

Finger foods, as their very name suggests, are easy to serve. All too often this means that they get short shrift when it comes to presentation: just plunk them down and let guests pick them up. But the very ease with which finger foods are served allows you more time to be creative in their presentation, holding forth the promise of creating a truly memorable party. By following a few simple principles of planning, cooking and serving finger foods, you'll ensure both yourself and your guests a great time.

One of the earliest steps should be planning the menu. Consider the occasion—formal or informal, daytime or evening, time of year. Then think about the ingredients in season at the market, along with your guests' likes, dislikes or dietary needs. The results of these decisions should offer some clear guidelines you can use to select specific recipes. Be sure, as well, to aim for a well-rounded menu, composed of dishes that vary in their ingredients, seasonings, colors and shapes—unless, of course, the theme of your party, such as a seafood extravaganza, demands particular choices.

Your attention should then turn to strategizing the event. Using the ingredients lists of the recipes you want to make, compile a master shopping list, checking your pantry for foods you already have in stock and those you need to replenish. Draw up a separate list of special stops you might have to make, at a fish market, for example, or a good bakery. Also think about any ready to serve finger foods you might like to add, such as a selection of cheeses and crackers, and any attractive items you could use to line or garnish the platters, from paper doilies to colorful, distinctively shaped salad leaves.

With your recipes in hand, now is a good time to consider what you will serve them in. Finger foods lend themselves to presentation on platters or trays. Pull from your shelves the appropriate serving pieces and select for each recipe one or more that will best complement its colors and shapes. You might also use other flat surfaces, such as marble pastry slabs, wooden cutting boards or shallow straw baskets. Bowls of various sizes can come in handy for heaps of potato chips, onion rings, nuts, olives or spreads.

For a small gathering, one platter or tray will more than suffice for each recipe. In some cases, two or more recipes could share a large serving dish. As the size of your party grows, and you need to multiply the yield of your recipes, more ingenuity is required. Two dishes per recipe—one set out for guests to help themselves, the other left in the kitchen to be replenished—make the food flow more efficiently. Foods meant to be eaten hot can be presented on an electrically heated serving tray. Alternatively, you can preheat serving ware and set it on an attractive heatproof pad or trivet.

Before the day of the party, give some creative thought to precisely where you will arrange your platters of finger food. The dining table is the most obvious choice, but take the time to scout your home for other possible settings. A coffee table, a captain's table by the fire, stand-alone snack trays, a deep windowsill or bench in a bay window, a kitchen table or counter away from the action of food preparation—any flat surface can be pressed into service. Placing different platters in different locations can facilitate the flow of your party and help avoid traffic jams that result when all the food is concentrated in

one spot. You should plan to have a separate table or counter, apart from the food, for cocktails, wine, beer, soft drinks and other beverages.

Wherever you place the food, plan on having stacks of napkins and small plates on which guests can place their selections, and hors d'oeuvre forks and toothpicks for those guests too fastidious to use their fingers. It's a wise host who sets out at least twice as many plates, napkins and utensils as there will be guests, assuming that people will lose track of their plates and start afresh at some point during the party. If the gathering will be large, don't shy away from using disposable items. Many stores sell very sturdy, attractive products suitable for the most elegant event.

A few days before your party, go over your lists again and add any items that will complement the atmosphere you wish to create. Candlelight, for example, lends a touch of magic to any occasion, whether you use chunky votives for the holidays or elegant tapers for a formal affair. Flowers or other centerpieces can complement the colors and shapes of the food. Music plays its part, whether you add a lively reggae beat to a poolside party of hot-weather finger foods or use classical strings to set the mood for the appetizers served at an intimate rendezvous for two.

MENUS

Gathering of Sports Fans

SERVES 6–8

When friends get together around the television to watch a favorite sports event, you don't want food preparation to take you away from the action. The best solution is to set out a selection of snacks that can be guided effortlessly from guest to guest, and go well with beer or soft drinks. A modicum of advance work is required and the final cooking can easily be done a few minutes before game time.

❧

Cocktail-Size Chilies Rellenos

Beer-Battered Onion Rings

Potato Wedges with Chili Aïoli

Chicken, Chili and Avocado Tostaditas

Make-Ahead Picnic

SERVES 6

When the weather warms up and the sun rules the sky, one of life's great pleasures is eating with family and friends al fresco—whether in a favorite local park, at the beach, in an open-air theater or out in the countryside. Picnic preparations can all too often threaten to overwhelm the inherent simplicity and spontaneity of such an occasion. Choose from a selection of foods that are easily made in advance and refrigerated, packed neatly in airtight containers in an insulated cooler and—best of all—eaten without utensils, and you have a picnic in the very best sense of the word. Just be sure to bring along napkins, paper or plastic plates, your drinks of choice and, of course, a large blanket to spread on the ground.

❧

Crudités with Lemon-Dill Vinaigrette

Stuffed Eggs with Tarragon

Dolmas

Smoked Salmon Lavash Rolls

Easy Cocktail Party

SERVES 6

The cocktail party has returned resoundingly to fashion. Held in the early evening—its hour or two duration clearly indicating that it wraps up before dinner—it provides an easy and enjoyable way to host friends or colleagues without preparing a full-scale meal. Cocktail entertaining becomes all the easier when the menu consists of dishes that can readily be made ahead. You needn't even stock a full bar. Just confine beverages to wine, beer and sparkling water, or make one classic cocktail, such as the martini, the main attraction.

Toasted Spicy Nuts

Spiced Olives

Corn Cups with Tomato-Corn Salsa

Desert Flat Bread with assorted cheese spreads

Smoked Salmon Lavash Rolls

Bite-Sized Barbecue

SERVES 8

One of the most cunning ways a host could entertain is to let the guests do a good part of the work themselves. That's the secret behind this menu. You do the simple preparation: cutting up the ingredients, marinating them, threading the skewers for the shrimp and pork brochettes (doubling the recipes to allow two servings per guest). Half an hour or so before guests arrive, build a fire in a charcoal grill. When you make the caponata a day or two ahead, grilling the eggplant and assembling the quesadillas can easily be completed before the party. All that's left to do is set out platters of ready-to-grill food and a selection of chilled beverages. Then, turn guests loose for a casual party everyone will enjoy.

Vegetable Bruschetta

Grilled Eggplant Topped with Caponata

Grilled Shrimp Wrapped in Bacon and Basil

Spanish Pork Brochettes

assorted breads for accompaniment

Dim Sum Buffet

SERVES 6–8

"Delight the heart" is how the Chinese term *dim sum* is usually translated. Small dumplings and other bites of food traditionally served as a morning meal, dim sum have become in the West favorite lunchtime treats and novel foods to serve with beer or wine when entertaining in the early evening. Imbued with a Pan-Asian spirit, the dim sum offerings of many innovative restaurants include specialties from countries other than China—a practice that makes this particular menu especially delightful. Be sure to provide chopsticks for guests who don't wish to use their fingers.

Oysters with Pickled Ginger, Daikon and Lime

Shrimp Puffs with Sesame Seeds

Chicken Slivers with Chipotle-Peanut Sauce

Rice Paper Dumplings

Crisp Fried Spring Rolls

Mediterranean Open House

SERVES 8

Whether the occasion is a family reunion, a shower, a homecoming or a housewarming, celebrating with an open house calls for a casual mood that encourages guests to come and go as they please, enjoying the gathering at their leisure. What better cuisines to provide the menu for this style of entertaining than those of the Mediterranean. Plates and linens in bright, lively patterns can complement the sunny colors and vivid tastes of these finger foods. Add appropriate music, be it Spanish flamenco, French ballads, Italian operettas or Greek bouzouki. Offer drinks that suit the event and personal tastes, from sherry to sangria, Chianti to ouzo.

Spanokopita

Dolmas

Italian Bread Dipped in Oil and Sage

Anchovy and Onion Tart

Roasted Tomato Hearts

Fried Calamari with Lemon Aioli

Holiday by the Fire

SERVES 8–10

At no time of year do we seem to entertain more than during the final two months. Chilly temperatures make such gatherings all the more cozy, providing an excuse to stoke the fireplace and make it the focal point of a casual change of pace from the season's sit-down meals. The finger foods below, though easy to prepare, serve and eat, have a robust, warming character and a special festive air. For a menu that serves up to 10, you'll want to double the recipes for Crab Cakes and Scallion Biscuits. Stir up a punch bowl of eggnog, or mull some wine or ale on the stove. Then break out your best holiday tableware or, for faster cleanup, buy disposable plates and napkins in seasonal colors and patterns.

✿

Red Pepper Puttanesca Canapés

Creamy Chicken Canapés

Scallion Biscuits with Smoked Salmon Spread

Piroshki

Crab Cakes

Black-Tie Affair

SERVES 8

Wearing formal attire transforms any occasion, be it New Year's Eve, a gathering before the theater or opera, or a reception for a special guest. Conversation sparkles, assisted by the gleam of your best crystal and silver, the twinkle of candlelight and the effervescence of champagne. The finger foods you serve should match the occasion in elegance. Offering refined ingredients and tastes, they will set such an elevated tone that you and your guests may not have to dress up at all! To serve 8, triple the recipe for Shrimp-Filled Salmon Cones.

✿

Parmesan Cheese Biscuits

Shrimp-Filled Salmon Cones

Roasted Tomato Hearts

Spinach Pancakes with Sour Cream and Salmon Roe

Wild Mushroom Filo Packets

WRAPPED, ROLLED & STUFFED

There's something cozy about the finger foods in this chapter. Snugly enclosed in pastry or pasta or in their own natural containers, they strike instant associations with our own inclinations to nest, to tuck ourselves in.

That comfortableness helps set an agreeably casual tone when such appetizers are served at a party. Home-style ethnic favorites like Eastern European piroshki, Greek spanokopita, Asian spring rolls or miniature Mexican chilies rellenos put guests pleasurably at their ease—not least because such finger foods are so neat and effortless to eat. They can also take on more elegant airs. Stuff mushroom caps with succulent crabmeat or roll strips of smoked salmon around a horseradish-seasoned shrimp filling, and you have finger food worthy of a black-tie affair.

Whether the tone you aim to set when entertaining is formal or laid-back, wrapped, rolled and stuffed finger foods can be assembled well in advance and even arranged ahead of time on their serving platters. Compact and self-contained as they are, these finger foods also pack efficiently when the occasion takes you to a venue away from home—be it a picnic in the park, a potluck gathering at a friend's house or an open-air summertime concert beneath the stars.

Dolmas (recipe page 44)

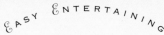

PIROSHKI

Russian and Polish hosts most often serve these meat-filled turnovers with borscht. Presented on their own, Piroshki *make a perfect companion to iced vodka or chilled beer. Feel free to vary the filling ingredients, using ground pork, turkey or chicken, for example, instead of the beef or fish, or seasoning with another favorite herb. Because the* Piroshki *are good at room temperature, you can bake them up to 1 hour ahead.*

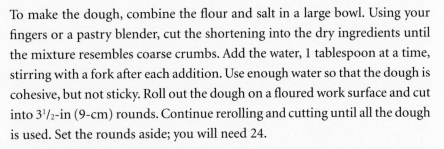

3 cups (15 oz/465 g) all-purpose (plain) flour

1 teaspoon salt

1 cup (8 oz/250 g) vegetable shortening (vegetable lard)

7–8 tablespoons (about 4 fl oz/ 125 ml) water

2 tablespoons butter

1 onion, chopped

1/3 lb (5 oz/155 g) ground (minced) beef or cooked, flaked fish

1 hard-boiled (hard-cooked) egg, chopped

2 tablespoons chopped fresh dill

1/2 cup (4 fl oz/125 ml) sour cream

salt and freshly ground pepper

To make the dough, combine the flour and salt in a large bowl. Using your fingers or a pastry blender, cut the shortening into the dry ingredients until the mixture resembles coarse crumbs. Add the water, 1 tablespoon at a time, stirring with a fork after each addition. Use enough water so that the dough is cohesive, but not sticky. Roll out the dough on a floured work surface and cut into 3 1/2-in (9-cm) rounds. Continue rerolling and cutting until all the dough is used. Set the rounds aside; you will need 24.

To make the filling, melt the butter in a medium sauté pan over low heat. Add the onion and cook gently for about 5 minutes. Transfer to a medium bowl. If you are using ground beef, cook the meat in the same pan over medium heat until it loses its pinkness, breaking it up with a spatula as it cooks. Add it to the onion. If you are using cooked fish, simply combine it with the onion. Add the egg, dill and sour cream and toss gently to combine. Season to taste with salt and pepper. The mixture should be moist, but not runny.

Preheat an oven to 425°F (220°C). Brush the edges of each circle of dough with water and place a heaping teaspoon of filling on one side. Fold the dough over and press the edges firmly with the tines of a fork to seal. Prick the top of each turnover twice with a fork. Place the turnovers on an ungreased baking sheet and bake until golden, about 20 minutes. Serve warm or at room temperature.

MAKES 24 TURNOVERS

❼ SPANOKOPITA

1 lb (500 g) spinach

2 tablespoons olive oil, plus olive oil for brushing

12 green (spring) onions, chopped, including some tender green tops

³/₄ lb (375 g) feta cheese

¹/₄ cup (¹/₃ oz/10 g) chopped fresh parsley

¹/₄ cup (¹/₃ oz/10 g) chopped fresh dill

pinch of freshly grated nutmeg

freshly ground pepper

14 filo sheets

Everyone knows and loves these rich, bite-sized Greek pies, with their flaky filo crust and dill-scented spinach filling. For another interesting presentation, spoon a thin line of filling lengthwise along one edge of the stacked filo strips, then roll up into a thin tube and coil like a snail. Once shaped, the triangles or coils may be frozen before baking, layered between waxed paper to prevent sticking.

Stem the spinach, chop it into small pieces or cut into shreds and wash it well to remove all traces of sand. Drain and dry thoroughly. In a large sauté pan over medium heat, warm the 2 tablespoons olive oil. Add the spinach and onions and sauté until the spinach wilts and cooks down, about 5 minutes. Drain well, pressing out as much liquid as possible. Chop coarsely and set aside.

In a medium bowl, mash the feta cheese with a fork. Add the spinach-onion mixture, parsley, dill and nutmeg. Mix well and season to taste with pepper.

Preheat an oven to 375°F (190°C). Brush a 10¹/₂-by-16-by-2¹/₂-in (26-by-40-by-6-cm) pan with olive oil. Lay the filo sheets on a clean, dry work surface and cut lengthwise into long strips 3 in (7.5 cm) wide. For each triangle stack 2 or 3 strips, brushing each strip with olive oil before adding the next. Place a heaping tablespoon of filling near one end and fold over the filo to form a triangle. Continue folding as you would a flag. Arrange on the pan, cover and refrigerate for about 30 minutes.

Bake the triangles until golden, about 30 minutes. Let rest for 5–10 minutes before serving.

MAKES 16–20 TRIANGLES

CRAB-STUFFED MUSHROOMS

The natural sweetness of crabmeat makes it an ideal stuffing for rich, earthy-tasting mushrooms. Be sure to pass these with plenty of napkins, as the baked morsels will be very juicy. For a fresh summertime variation, try mixing a simple salad of cooked crabmeat, mayonnaise, minced shallot and fresh herbs, spooning it into medium to large raw button mushroom caps.

Preheat an oven to 425°F (220°C). In a food processor fitted with the metal blade, process the $^1/_2$ cup morels and the white button mushrooms and lemon juice until minced.

In a large sauté pan, melt the butter over medium-high heat. Add the minced mushrooms, celery, onion, garlic and green onion. Cook, stirring often, until almost all the liquid has evaporated, 2–3 minutes. Add the cream and cook until reduced by half, lowering the heat as needed. Add the crabmeat and cook until almost all the liquid has evaporated, 1–3 minutes. Remove from the heat and stir in the salt, Tabasco sauce, parsley, cheese and as much of the bread crumbs as needed to make a cohesive mixture. Set aside to cool.

Stuff the mushroom halves with the mixture, dividing it evenly among them. Sprinkle the tops with some of the leftover bread crumbs. Place mushrooms in a single layer in a baking dish. Pour the white wine around the mushrooms and bake until they are tender, 14–17 minutes. Serve immediately.

MAKES 24–30 STUFFED MUSHROOMS

$^1/_2$ cup (2 oz) coarsely chopped morel mushrooms, plus 12–15 large morel mushrooms, cut in half and stemmed

1 cup (4 oz/125 g) coarsely chopped white button (cultivated) mushrooms

4 teaspoons fresh lemon juice

$^1/_4$ cup (2 oz/60 g) butter

$^1/_4$ cup (1$^1/_2$ oz/45 g) minced celery

$^1/_4$ cup (1$^1/_2$ oz/45 g) minced onion

1 tablespoon minced garlic

1 large green (spring) onion, minced

$^3/_4$ cup (6 fl oz/180 ml) heavy (double) cream

8 oz (250 g) fresh or frozen Dungeness crabmeat

$^1/_4$ teaspoon salt

dash of Tabasco (hot red pepper) sauce

3 tablespoons minced fresh parsley

$^1/_3$ cup (1$^1/_2$ oz/45 g) grated Parmesan cheese

$^1/_2$ cup (2 oz/60 g) dried bread crumbs, or more as needed

$^1/_2$ cup (4 fl oz/125 ml) dry white wine

WILD MUSHROOM FILO PACKETS

Headily aromatic with garlic, thyme and paprika, the mushroom-and-egg filling for these crisp filo rectangles goes wonderfully with a glass of white wine or beer. You can use any variety of fresh mushrooms available at your local market: chanterelles, morels, porcini, portobellos, cremini, shiitakes or even ordinary white button mushrooms.

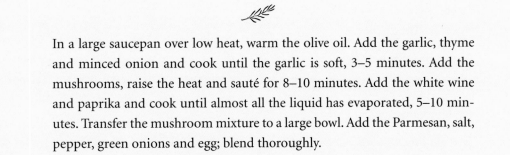

3 tablespoons olive oil

1 tablespoon minced garlic

1 tablespoon chopped fresh thyme or 1 teaspoon dried thyme

2 tablespoons minced onion

2 lb (1 kg) sliced mixed wild mushrooms

1/2 cup (4 fl oz/125 ml) dry white wine

1 teaspoon paprika

1 cup (4 oz/125 g) freshly grated Parmesan cheese

1 teaspoon salt

1/2 teaspoon freshly ground black pepper

1 cup (3 oz/90 g) sliced green (spring) onions

1 egg

28–30 filo sheets

1/2 cup (4 oz/125 g) butter, melted

In a large saucepan over low heat, warm the olive oil. Add the garlic, thyme and minced onion and cook until the garlic is soft, 3–5 minutes. Add the mushrooms, raise the heat and sauté for 8–10 minutes. Add the white wine and paprika and cook until almost all the liquid has evaporated, 5–10 minutes. Transfer the mushroom mixture to a large bowl. Add the Parmesan, salt, pepper, green onions and egg; blend thoroughly.

Preheat an oven to 375°F (190°C). Lightly oil 2 baking sheets. Cut the filo sheets into rectangles measuring 8 by 12 in (20 by 30 cm). Place a rectangle on a clean, dry work surface, brush lightly with the melted butter, place a second sheet on top and brush it lightly. Spoon 2 tablespoons of the mushroom filling on the filo about 2 in (5 cm) from one short edge, centered between the long edges. Fold each long edge toward the center, overlapping the edges slightly and enclosing the filling. Fold the nearer short edge over the filling, then continue folding the rectangle containing the filling to take up the remaining dough. The rectangle should measure approximately 2 by 3 1/2 in (5 by 9 cm). Repeat until all the filling and filo dough have been used.

Place the packets, flap down, on the baking sheets. Brush the remaining melted butter over the packets. Bake until golden brown and crisp, 10–15 minutes. Serve warm or at room temperature.

MAKES 28–30 PACKETS

Top to bottom: Crab-Stuffed Mushrooms (recipe page 29), Wild Mushroom Filo Packets

RICE PAPER DUMPLINGS

1 tablespoon vegetable oil

8 oz (250 g) ground (minced) pork

$^1/_2$ cup (2 oz/60 g) ground
roasted peanuts

4 cloves garlic, minced

$^1/_4$ cup ($^1/_3$ oz/10 g) chopped fresh
cilantro (fresh coriander)

$^1/_2$ teaspoon white pepper

3 tablespoons fish sauce *(nam pla)*

2 tablespoons sugar

$^1/_4$ cup (2 fl oz/60 ml) vegetable oil

6 cloves garlic, chopped

24 Thai rice paper sheets

24 lettuce leaves

$^1/_2$ cup ($^2/_3$ oz/20 g) fresh cilantro
(fresh coriander) leaves

Delicate yet bursting with flavor, these little half-moon-shaped dumplings—a popular snack from the street markets of Bangkok—are easily made by enfolding the cooked, aromatic filling in translucent circles of softened, edible rice paper. You'll find packages of rice paper in Asian markets and the Asian food section of well-stocked supermarkets. If you like, substitute ground chicken for the pork.

To make the filling, in a medium sauté pan over medium-high heat, warm the 1 tablespoon vegetable oil. Add the pork, peanuts, minced garlic, cilantro, white pepper, fish sauce and sugar. Cook until the pork is thoroughly done and the liquid is reduced. Set the filling aside.

In a small sauté pan over medium heat, warm the $^1/_4$ cup (2 fl oz/60 ml) vegetable oil. Add the chopped garlic and cook until golden, 5–6 minutes. Discard the garlic and reserve the oil.

To prepare the dumplings, fill a large stockpot with water to a depth of 2–3 in (5–7.5 cm) and set a steamer basket or rack in the pot. Moisten each sheet of rice paper and cut into circles 5 in (12.5 cm) in diameter. Working in batches, steam the circles for 1–2 minutes and place on a plate with a layer of plastic wrap between them. Spoon 1 teaspoon of the filling on each rice paper circle. Fold the rice paper in half to cover the filling. Overlap and crimp the edges to shape and seal each dumpling. Brush each dumpling with the garlic oil. Repeat with the remaining rice paper circles and filling.

Arrange the lettuce leaves on a serving platter. Place the dumplings on the leaves and garnish with the cilantro leaves. Guests pick up the dumplings by wrapping them in the lettuce leaves.

MAKES 24 DUMPLINGS

Left to right: Crisp Fried Spring Rolls (recipe page 36), Fresh Thai Spring Rolls

2/3 cup (5 fl oz/160 ml) coconut
  milk

1 tablespoon red curry paste
  (*nam prik gaeng ped*)

2 tablespoons fish sauce (*nam pla*)

1 1/2 tablespoons sugar

1/2 cup (4 oz/125 g) ground
  roasted peanuts

12 spring roll wrappers

12 lettuce leaves, cut into 6-in
  (15-cm) squares

3 Chinese sausages, cut into
  1/2-in (1-cm) strips

1 cup (8 oz/250 g) fried tofu

1 cucumber, peeled and cut into
  1/2-in (1-cm) strips

2 cups (8 oz/250 g) bean sprouts,
  blanched

2 cups (2 oz/60 g) spinach,
  blanched

FRESH THAI SPRING ROLLS

Eaten fresh, not fried, these traditional Bangkok-style spring rolls are ideal for health-conscious guests, or when entertaining on a hot day. In place of the Chinese sausages, which are available in Asian markets, you can use 3 to 4 dozen cooked medium-sized shrimp. The rolls may be prepared several hours in advance, arranged on a serving tray in a single layer, covered with plastic wrap and refrigerated.

To make the peanut sauce, combine the coconut milk, red curry paste, fish sauce, sugar and ground peanuts in a medium saucepan and simmer for 15 minutes, stirring constantly. Set aside.

To make the spring rolls, fill a large stockpot with water to a depth of 2–3 in (5–7.5 cm) and set a steamer basket or rack in the pot. Working in batches, steam the spring roll wrappers for 1–2 minutes and place on a plate with a layer of plastic wrap between them. Set the wrappers on a work surface and place a lettuce leaf on the lower portion of each wrapper. Evenly divide the sausage strips, fried tofu, cucumber strips, bean sprouts and blanched spinach among the lettuce-covered wrappers. Lift the bottom edge of each wrapper and roll up the wrappers, folding in the sides.

Cut the rolls into slices, if desired, and arrange on a serving platter, accompanied with the warm peanut sauce.

MAKES 12 ROLLS

CRISP FRIED SPRING ROLLS

Although they resemble Chinese spring rolls, these Thai favorites have an especially fragrant pork filling that sets them well apart from more familiar finger food. The rolls may be filled, covered and refrigerated several hours in advance of frying and serving.

2 tablespoons vegetable oil

1 teaspoon minced garlic

8 oz (250 g) ground (minced) pork

4 carrots, grated

4 celery stalks, grated

1/4 cup (2 fl oz/60 ml) fish sauce (*nam pla*)

1 tablespoon Worcestershire sauce

2 tablespoons sugar

1/8 teaspoon white pepper

1 cup (4 oz/125 g) bean sprouts

20 spring roll wrappers

2 egg yolks, beaten

vegetable oil for deep-frying

To make the filling, in a large sauté pan over medium heat, warm the 2 tablespoons vegetable oil. Add the garlic and pork and sauté until the pork is thoroughly cooked. Add the carrots, celery, fish sauce, Worcestershire sauce, sugar and pepper. Cook over high heat until the sauce is reduced, 1–2 minutes. Drain any remaining liquid from the pan. Set the filling aside to cool, then stir in the bean sprouts.

To prepare the spring rolls, working in batches, set a wrapper on a work surface with a corner facing you, so that the wrapper resembles a diamond. Place 2 tablespoons of the filling in the lower portion of the wrapper. Fold up the lower corner, bring the 2 sides into the center and brush the upper portion of the wrapper with the egg yolks. Roll up the wrapper to seal the filling. Fill and fold the remaining wrappers.

In a large, heavy skillet, pour vegetable oil to a depth of 2–3 in (5–7.5 cm). Heat the oil to 350°F (180°C). When the oil is the correct temperature, a cube of bread dropped in the oil will brown in 1 minute. Deep-fry the spring rolls in batches until golden brown on all sides, turning as needed. Transfer the rolls to paper towels to drain. Cut in slices, if desired, and arrange on a serving platter.

MAKES 20 ROLLS

SMOKED SALMON LAVASH ROLLS

2 lavash rounds, each about 12 in (30 cm) in diameter

²/₃ cup (5 fl oz/160 ml) mayonnaise

2 teaspoons chopped fresh dill or pinch of dried dill

freshly ground pepper

finely grated zest of 1 lemon

8 oz (250 g) thinly sliced cold-smoked salmon

Lavash, a thin, traditionally crisp bread, is the oldest form of bread found in the Middle East. Available in ethnic markets and well-stocked supermarkets, it can be moistened to make it soft and pliable, allowing you to roll it up around a filling and then slice it into bite-sized rounds. In this recipe, you could substitute softened cream cheese for the mayonnaise. (photograph page 48)

Gently rinse each lavash round under cold running water for about 10 seconds on each side. Place on a damp, clean towel and cover with another damp, clean towel. Let stand for 1 hour to soften.

In a small bowl, stir together the mayonnaise, dill, pepper to taste and lemon zest until well mixed. Remove the lavash from the towels and place each round on a sheet of plastic wrap. Spread the mayonnaise mixture evenly over the rounds. Cover with the salmon slices in a single layer. Using the plastic wrap to lift up the edge of the bread, roll up each round firmly but not tightly. Cover with plastic wrap and refrigerate for about 1 hour or up to 2 days before serving.

To serve, cut each roll crosswise into 12 slices about 1 in (2.5 cm) thick.

MAKES 24 ROLLS

*Top to bottom: Roasted Tomato Hearts (recipe page 50), Parmesan Cheese Biscuits
(recipe page 76), Cocktail Pasties with Tomato Sauce*

COCKTAIL PASTIES WITH TOMATO SAUCE

Out of England by way of Australia, these robust little meat and vegetable turn-overs bring a touch of class to what once served as lunch for coal miners. Try them with ground lamb, pork or turkey instead of the beef. They're so moist and flavorful that you don't even need the tomato sauce, though it's so easy and so good that you may wind up serving it with everything.

10 whole cloves

1 piece fresh ginger, about $^1/_3$ oz (10 g)

1 tablespoon whole allspice

12 tomatoes, chopped

$^2/_3$ cup (5 oz/155 g) sugar

salt and freshly ground pepper

$1^1/_4$ cups (10 fl oz/310 ml) malt vinegar

2 green (spring) onions, chopped

1 small clove garlic, chopped

$3^1/_2$ oz (105 g) lean ground (minced) beef

$^1/_2$ onion, coarsely grated

2 small carrots, coarsely grated

1 small zucchini (courgette), coarsely grated

$^1/_2$ celery stalk, coarsely grated

1 small potato, peeled and coarsely grated

2 tablespoons frozen peas, thawed

6 frozen puff pastry sheets, each 10 in (25 cm) square, thawed

1 egg yolk, beaten with 2 teaspoons water

To make the sauce, place the cloves, ginger and allspice in a small square of cheesecloth, bring together the corners and tie securely with kitchen twine. Place the cloth bag, tomatoes, sugar, salt to taste, vinegar, green onions and garlic in a large, heavy saucepan and bring slowly to a boil. Cover the pot and simmer over low heat until the mixture has thickened, $1^1/_2$ hours. Let the sauce cool, then discard the cloth bag. Strain the sauce to remove the skins and seeds. You should have about $1^1/_4$ cups (10 fl oz/310 ml).

While the sauce cooks, preheat an oven to 400°F (200°C). Butter 2 baking sheets. To make the pasties, combine the beef, grated onion, carrots, zucchini, celery, potato and peas in a large bowl. Season to taste with salt and pepper and mix well. Separate the pastry sheets and, working in batches if necessary, arrange on a work surface. Using a sharp knife, cut out 4 rounds, each 4 in (10 cm) in diameter. Spoon an equal portion of the filling into the center of each pastry round, leaving a $^3/_4$-in (2-cm) uncovered border around the edges. Dampen the uncovered edges with cold water and fold each round in half. Press the edges firmly with the tines of a fork to seal.

Arrange the pasties on the baking sheets. Brush the tops with the egg yolk mixture. Bake until puffed and golden, about 18 minutes. Let rest for 5 minutes. Serve warm or at room temperature, accompanied with the sauce.

MAKES 24 PASTIES

STUFFED EGGS WITH TARRAGON

Different from mustard-flavored deviled eggs, these stuffed egg halves present a surprisingly harmonious blend of individually distinctive tastes: fresh tarragon, tuna, capers and fruity extra-virgin olive oil. Once stuffed, the eggs may be held in the refrigerator for up to 3 hours, loosely covered with plastic wrap.

6 hard-boiled (hard-cooked) eggs

2 tablespoons minced fresh tarragon or fresh parsley

2 tablespoons extra-virgin olive oil

1 tablespoon capers in wine vinegar, drained and chopped

2 tablespoons canned tuna in olive oil, drained

salt and freshly ground pepper

Cut the eggs in half lengthwise and remove the yolks. Place the yolks in a small bowl. Cut a very thin slice off the rounded base of each egg white half so that it lays flat. Set the whites aside.

Add the tarragon or parsley, olive oil, capers and tuna to the egg yolks. Mash the ingredients together with a fork to form a smooth mixture. Season to taste with salt and pepper. Spoon the yolk mixture into the reserved egg white halves. Serve chilled or at room temperature.

MAKES 12 STUFFED EGGS

STUFFED MUSSELS ON THE HALF SHELL

With their egg-sized, gleaming blue-black shells, mussels make ideal finger-food containers, their plump, sweet flesh highlighted by garlic, tomatoes and crisp bread crumbs. In this recipe, sausage is also included in the mixture; feel free to leave it out if you'd prefer a lighter version.

7 oz (220 g) sweet Italian sausages, skinned and crumbled

2 tablespoons chopped fresh parsley

2 cloves garlic, chopped

2 plum (Roma) tomatoes, peeled and chopped

1 egg

3 tablespoons fine dried bread crumbs

salt

5 lb (2.5 kg) large mussels, scrubbed and debearded

2 tablespoons extra-virgin olive oil

In a medium bowl, combine the sausage, parsley, garlic, tomatoes, egg and 2 tablespoons of the bread crumbs. Season to taste with salt and mix well. Place the mussels in a shallow saucepan, cover and set over medium heat until the shells open, about 5 minutes. Remove from the heat and discard any that did not open. Open the mussels and discard the top shells. Loosen the mussel meats from the bottom shells and leave them nestled in the shells.

Preheat an oven to 350°F (180°C). Divide the sausage mixture among the mussels, mounding it on top. Sprinkle with the remaining 1 tablespoon bread crumbs and the olive oil. Arrange the mussels on a flat ovenproof pan. Bake for 15 minutes. Serve very hot.

MAKES ABOUT 50 STUFFED MUSSELS

Top to bottom: Green Chili Corn Cakes with Caviar (recipe page 57),
Shrimp-Filled Salmon Cones

3/4 lb (375 g) cooked tiny (bay)
   shrimp

3/4 cup (6 fl oz/180 ml) heavy
   (double) cream, whipped

2 teaspoons minced fresh dill

1 tablespoon prepared horseradish

salt and freshly ground
   white pepper

6 thin slices cold-smoked salmon

2 tablespoons salmon roe,
   for garnish *(optional)*

6 fresh dill sprigs for garnish

2 lemons, cut into wedges,
   for garnish

SHRIMP-FILLED SALMON CONES

Taking their inspiration from the ham and cream cheese rolls popular in the 1950s, these luxurious mouthfuls up the ante on elegance with wrappers of smoked salmon and a filling combining bay shrimp and horseradish cream. As smoked salmon is the star attraction, be sure to buy the very best quality you can find. The rolls may be made, covered and refrigerated up to several hours in advance.

In a medium bowl, combine the shrimp, whipped cream, minced dill and horseradish. Season lightly with salt and white pepper.

Spread the shrimp filling on the smoked salmon slices and roll each slice into a cone shape. Garnish with the salmon roe (if desired), dill sprigs and lemon wedges. Serve chilled or at room temperature.

MAKES 6 ROLLS

DOLMAS

Rice-stuffed grape leaves are an essential part of any Turkish or Greek meze, or appetizer, assortment. You could use the same stuffing to fill other bite-sized containers such as mussels or small tomatoes or zucchini. For a meat filling, reduce the rice to $^1/_2$ cup ($3^1/_2$ oz/110 g), omit the tomatoes and mint or dill, and add $^1/_2$ lb (250 g) ground lamb. (photograph pages 24–25)

1 cup (7 oz/220 g) long-grain rice

3 tablespoons olive oil

2 onions, chopped

3 cloves garlic, minced

$^1/_2$ teaspoon ground cinnamon

$^1/_2$ teaspoon ground allspice

$^2/_3$ cup (4 oz/125 g) peeled, seeded and diced tomatoes

$^1/_2$ cup ($2^1/_2$ oz/75 g) pine nuts, toasted

$^1/_2$ cup (3 oz/90 g) dried currants, plumped in hot water to cover and drained

2 tablespoons chopped fresh parsley

2 tablespoons chopped fresh mint or dill

salt and freshly ground pepper

36 bottled grape leaves, rinsed of brine, well drained and stemmed

1 cup (8 fl oz/250 ml) olive oil

2–3 tablespoons fresh lemon juice

Place the rice in a small bowl with water to cover. Let stand for 30 minutes. Drain. In a medium sauté pan over medium heat, warm 3 tablespoons olive oil. Add the onions and sauté, stirring occasionally, until tender and translucent, about 10 minutes. Add the garlic, cinnamon and allspice and sauté for 3 minutes. Transfer to a large bowl. Add the drained rice, tomatoes, pine nuts, currants, parsley, mint or dill, and salt and pepper to taste. Mix well.

Lay the grape leaves flat on a work surface. Place a teaspoon of the filling near the stem end of the leaf. Fold the stem end over the filling, fold the sides over the filling, then roll the leaf into a cylinder. Do not roll too tightly, as the rice will expand in cooking. Repeat with the remaining grape leaves and filling.

Arrange the Dolmas, seam sides down, in a large, wide sauté pan. Pour the 1 cup (8 fl oz/250 ml) olive oil and the lemon juice over the Dolmas. Add enough hot water to cover by 1 in (2.5 cm). Weight down with a large, round plate. Bring to a boil, cover, reduce the heat to low and simmer until the filling is cooked, 45–50 minutes.

Immediately, uncover the pan so the Dolmas cool quickly, then transfer to a serving platter. The Dolmas can be stored in a covered container in the refrigerator for up to 3 days and brought to room temperature before serving.

MAKES 36 DOLMAS

❧ COCKTAIL-SIZE CHILIES RELLENOS

1 cup (5 oz/155 g) unbleached
all-purpose (plain) flour

1 teaspoon salt

1 cup (8 fl oz/250 ml) beer

5 Anaheim or New Mexico green
chilies, roasted, peeled, seeded
and cut into ³/₄-in (2-cm) strips

4 oz (125 g) Monterey Jack cheese,
cut into ³/₄-by-¹/₂-by-¹/₂-in
(2-cm-by-12-mm-by-12 mm)
pieces and chilled

vegetable oil for frying

A miniature version of the batter-coated, cheese-stuffed green chilies so popular in Mexico and the American Southwest, these are great cocktail-party fare and go especially well with Mexican beer. The yeast in the beer helps make the batter light and airy. (photograph pages 46–47)

In a large bowl, stir together the flour and salt. Add the beer and mix until smooth. Allow the batter to rest, covered, for 1 hour at room temperature.

Wrap a chili strip around each piece of cheese and secure with a toothpick. The cheese pieces can be prepared in advance and stored for 1 day in the refrigerator before using.

Fill a medium, heavy saucepan with oil to a depth of 1 in (2.5 cm). Heat to about 400°F (200°C). Dip the chili-covered cheese pieces in the batter, coating them well, and allow the excess to drip back into the bowl. Drop the batter-coated pieces in the hot oil and cook, turning once, until they are crisp and golden brown, 3–5 minutes. Remove from the hot oil with a slotted utensil and drain on paper towels. Repeat with the remaining cheese pieces and batter. Remove the toothpicks and serve immediately.

MAKES ABOUT 20 CHILIES RELLENOS

NACHOS & CANAPÉS

Breads in all their variety—from small slices of rustic Italian loaves to fresh-baked biscuits, from crisp tortilla chips to flat Middle Eastern pita and lavash—provide perfect foundations for finger foods. Top them with cheese, salsa, cooked vegetables, seafood or poultry, and you have party food at once reassuringly familiar and beguilingly different.

That familiarity no doubt traces back to the lunch boxes or bags we all carried as schoolchildren. Call these recipes what you will—nachos, bruschetta, quesadillas, canapés. In essence, they're all morsel-sized sandwiches. Yet, in the diversity suggested by their many different names, they intrigue with every bite.

Guests respond with gusto to such innovative creations. Nachos, for example, have become an overwhelmingly popular cocktail snack for the engaging way they combine the earthy taste of corn, the lively spice of salsa and the richness of cheese in a compact package. The principle still applies when you replace the corn chip with a crisply grilled round of baguette or a wedge of pita bread, and the Southwestern-style toppings with rapidly sautéed springtime vegetables or a heady mixture of anchovies, peppers, capers and olives.

Clockwise from left: Corn Cups with Tomato-Corn Salsa (recipe page 64), Chicken, Chili and Avocado Tostaditas (recipe page 65), Cocktail-Size Chilies Rellenos (recipe page 45)

SPINACH PANCAKES WITH SOUR CREAM AND SALMON ROE

If you want an elegant but inexpensive finger food to serve with champagne, look no further. Plump salmon eggs make as big an impression as far more costly caviar and have a luxurious taste reminiscent of smoked salmon. Their glistening, pinkish orange color looks stunning atop the green-flecked, bite-sized spinach pancakes. You could substitute beluga, osetra or sevruga caviars if you'd like to splurge.

Place the spinach in a colander and press out any excess water. In a medium bowl, combine the spinach, parsley and green onions. In a large bowl, beat the eggs. Add the 3 tablespoons milk, sour cream and melted butter and mix well. Stir in the flour, nutmeg and salt and pepper to taste. Fold in the spinach mixture. Let stand for 30 minutes.

In a large sauté pan (preferably nonstick) over medium heat, warm 1 tablespoon of the olive oil. Working in batches, spoon in 1 tablespoon of the spinach mixture to form each pancake; do not crowd the pan. Add more milk to the mixture if it seems too thick. Cook until the edges of the pancakes are golden, about 2 minutes. Flip the pancakes and cook until the second side is golden, about 2 minutes longer. Transfer to a serving plate and let cool. Repeat with the remaining oil and batter.

Top each cooled pancake with a spoonful of sour cream and then a spoonful of salmon roe. Serve at room temperature.

MAKES ABOUT 20 PANCAKES

½ lb (250 g) frozen chopped spinach, thawed

2 tablespoons minced fresh parsley

2 green (spring) onions, including tender green tops, finely chopped

2 eggs

3 tablespoons milk, or more as needed

3 tablespoons sour cream

1 tablespoon unsalted butter, melted

¾ cup (4 oz/125 g) plain (all-purpose) flour

pinch of freshly grated nutmeg

salt and freshly ground pepper

about ⅓ cup (3 fl oz/80 ml) olive oil

1 cup (8 oz/250 g) sour cream

6½ oz (200 g) salmon roe

Outside to center: Spinach Pancakes with Sour Cream and Salmon Roe, Smoked Salmon Lavash Rolls (recipe page 37)

3 frozen puff pastry sheets, each
   10 in (25 cm) square, thawed

3 tablespoons Dijon mustard

6 plum (Roma) tomatoes,
   thinly sliced

6–8 cherry tomatoes, sliced

fresh thyme sprigs for garnish

salt and freshly ground pepper

❧ ROASTED TOMATO HEARTS

Make these winning little savory pastries any time you want to show your guests that your heart is in the right place. Thanks to frozen puff pastry, they go together so quickly that it's hard to avoid improvising. Replace the mustard, for example, with commercially prepared pesto; use oregano instead of thyme; or add some small cubes of mozzarella or tissue-thin pieces of prosciutto to the tomatoes. (photograph page 38)

Preheat an oven to 425°F (220°C). Oil 2 baking sheets.

Lay the pastry sheets on a floured work surface. Using large and small heart-shaped cutters, stamp out hearts and arrange well spaced on the prepared trays. Spread each heart with some mustard and then top with a tomato slice; use larger slices on the large hearts and smaller ones on the small hearts.

Bake until the pastry is puffed and the tomatoes begin to color around the edges, 12–15 minutes. Arrange the hearts on a serving platter. Scatter with sprigs of thyme and season to taste with salt and pepper.

MAKES ABOUT 25 HEARTS

🌑 VEGETABLE BRUSCHETTA

A favorite Italian snack, bruschetta is nothing more than a crisped slice of good country bread simply topped with chopped fresh plum tomatoes or any of a wide array of more elaborate mixtures. Here, yellow bell pepper, yellow cherry tomatoes and asparagus join the plum tomatoes for an especially colorful effect.

3 tablespoons unsalted butter

2 tablespoons olive oil

1 yellow bell pepper (capsicum), seeded and cut into $3/4$-in (2-cm) dice

2 plum (Roma) tomatoes, diced

18 yellow cherry tomatoes, halved

$1/4$ lb (125 g) asparagus, cut into $3/8$-in (1-cm) pieces

2 teaspoons chopped fresh parsley

2 teaspoons balsamic vinegar

salt and freshly ground pepper

12 baguette slices, each $3/4$ in (2 cm) thick

2 cloves garlic, halved

Preheat a broiler (griller). In a large, heavy sauté pan over medium heat, melt the butter with the oil until sizzling. Add the bell pepper, plum and cherry tomatoes and asparagus and sauté until just tender, about 10 minutes. Stir in the parsley and vinegar and season to taste with salt and pepper. Remove from the heat and cover to keep warm. The vegetable mixture can be stored in a covered container in the refrigerator for up to 2 days. Warm over low heat before using.

Arrange the baguette slices on a baking sheet. Broil (grill) on both sides, turning once, until lightly golden. Rub one side with the cut garlic and arrange, garlic side up, on 1 or 2 platters. Spoon the hot vegetable mixture on top of the bread slices and serve at once.

MAKES 12 BRUSCHETTA

SCALLION BISCUITS WITH SMOKED SALMON SPREAD

1 small red (Spanish) onion, quartered lengthwise and thinly sliced crosswise

$^1/_4$ cup (2 fl oz/60 ml) seasoned rice vinegar

2 cups (10 oz/310 g) all-purpose (plain) flour

2 teaspoons baking powder

$1^1/_4$ teaspoons salt

$^1/_4$ teaspoon dry mustard

$^1/_4$ teaspoon freshly ground pepper

$^1/_3$ cup (3 oz/90 g) vegetable shortening (vegetable lard)

2 large green (spring) onions, minced

1 tablespoon minced fresh parsley

$^3/_4$ cup (6 fl oz/180 ml) plus $1^1/_2$ tablespoons milk

4 oz (125 g) cream cheese at room temperature

3 oz (90 g) thinly sliced cold-smoked salmon

$^1/_2$ teaspoon prepared horseradish

1 teaspoon fresh lemon juice

$^1/_2$ teaspoon minced fresh dill

Both biscuits and spread take only minutes to prepare, but their combined effect is so impressive that guests might think the effort took hours. The spread can be made up to 2 days in advance and kept covered in the refrigerator; let it come to room temperature before serving. If available, salmon roe makes a delicious garnish. Serve with iced vodka or champagne.

Preheat an oven to 425°F (220°C). Butter a baking sheet. In a small bowl, toss the onion and vinegar. Cover and set aside to marinate for at least 30 minutes or up to 3 hours.

To make the biscuits, sift the flour, baking powder, salt, dry mustard and black pepper into a large bowl. Cut in the shortening with a pastry blender or 2 knives, then stir in the green onions and parsley. Using a fork, lightly stir in enough milk to make a soft dough. Turn the dough out onto a lightly floured surface. Lightly pat the dough into a round $^3/_4$ in (2 cm) thick. Sprinkle with a little flour. Cut into 15 rounds with a $1^1/_2$-in (4-cm) biscuit cutter. Place the biscuits, sides touching, on the baking sheet. The biscuits can be prepared up to this point, then refrigerated up to 4 hours before baking. Bake until golden, 18–20 minutes. Let cool for about 10 minutes.

To make the spread, combine the cream cheese and half of the smoked salmon in a food processor fitted with the metal blade and process until smooth. Add the horseradish and lemon juice and process until smooth. Add the dill and process until incorporated. Transfer the spread to a small bowl. Mince the remaining salmon and stir it into the spread until blended.

Split the biscuits in half horizontally. Spread the bottoms with the salmon spread and top each with a little of the pickled onion. Arrange the biscuits on a serving platter, replace the tops and serve immediately.

MAKES 15 BISCUITS

Left to right: Scallion Biscuits with Smoked Salmon Spread,
Chilled Shrimp with Anise Mayonnaise (recipe page 91)

RED PEPPER PUTTANESCA CANAPÉS

2 red bell peppers (capsicums), roasted, peeled, seeded and cut into long strips $1/4$ in (6 mm) wide

6 anchovy fillets, drained and chopped into large pieces

$1^1/_2$ tablespoons well-drained capers

12 black olives, pitted and halved

2 teaspoons fresh oregano leaves

$1^1/_2$ tablespoons extra-virgin olive oil

freshly ground pepper

8 *pide* slices, each $^3/_8$ in (1 cm) thick

3 fresh parsley sprigs, stems removed and leaves chopped

Puttanesca, *an Italian word for a woman of easy virtue, vividly describes the coarse but undeniably appealing flavor combination of roasted bell peppers, anchovies, capers and olives. Warm* pide, *a Turkish flat bread topped with sesame seeds, serves as a base, but you could substitute slices of pita or seeded baguette. The pepper mixture can also be served in a bowl, with crisp slices of bread for dipping.*

Preheat a griller (broiler). In a small bowl, combine the bell peppers, anchovies, capers, olives, oregano, olive oil and pepper to taste. Mix well, taste and adjust the seasonings. The topping can be stored in a covered container in the refrigerator for 1–2 days. Bring to room temperature before using.

Arrange the *pide* slices on a baking sheet and broil (grill) on both sides, turning once, until just beginning to color. Arrange the slices on a platter. Spoon the pepper mixture on top of the slices and garnish with the parsley.

MAKES 8 CANAPÉS

Top to bottom: Red Pepper Puttanesca Canapés, Potato Wedges with Chili Aioli (recipe page 77), Grilled Eggplant Topped with Caponata (recipe page 56)

GRILLED EGGPLANT TOPPED WITH CAPONATA

Sicily's sweet-and-sour answer to ratatouille, caponata showcases a combination of eggplant, tomato, capers, olives, onion, anchovies and pine nuts. You could serve it in a bowl, with assorted crackers, breads and vegetables for dipping; use it as a filling for mushrooms; or, as here, spoon it onto grilled eggplant slices. Don't hesitate to make the caponata several days ahead and refrigerate it; the flavor improves with time.

2 large globe eggplants (aubergines), peeled and cut into ³/₄-in (2-cm) dice

salt and freshly ground pepper

³/₄ cup (6 fl oz/180 ml) olive oil

1 large onion, cut into slices ³/₈ in (1 cm) thick

12 fresh celery leaves

pinch of sugar, or to taste

¹/₃ cup (3 fl oz/80 ml) tomato paste (purée)

¹/₃ cup (3 fl oz/80 ml) white wine vinegar

1 tablespoon pine nuts

2 tablespoons chopped fresh oregano

3 tablespoons well-drained capers

²/₃ cup (3¹/₂ oz/105 g) pitted black olives, chopped

4 anchovy fillets, drained and roughly chopped

3 long, slender eggplants (aubergines), cut crosswise into slices ³/₈ in (1 cm) thick

4–5 tablespoons olive oil

To make the caponata, place the diced eggplant in a colander and salt liberally. Let stand for 30 minutes to drain off the bitter juices. Rinse off the salt under cold running water, squeeze by hand to remove excess water and pat dry with paper towels.

In a large, heavy sauté pan over medium heat, warm the ³/₄ cup (6 fl oz/180 ml) oil. Add the eggplant and cook, stirring, until softened, about 15 minutes. Transfer to a plate. Add the onion to the oil remaining in the pan and cook, stirring, until softened, about 5 minutes. Add the celery leaves, sugar and tomato paste and cook, stirring occasionally, for 5 minutes. Add the vinegar and cook over medium heat, stirring occasionally, until the mixture is reduced and thickened, about 10 minutes. Return the cooked eggplant to the pan and add the pine nuts, oregano, capers, olives and anchovies. Season to taste with salt and pepper, mix well and remove from the heat. Let cool.

To prepare the eggplant bases, preheat a broiler (griller). Arrange the eggplant slices on a baking sheet. Brush with about 2–3 tablespoons of the olive oil. Broil (grill) until just beginning to color, 2–3 minutes. Turn and brush the second side with the remaining olive oil and broil until tender, about 2 minutes longer; do not overcook. Transfer to a large platter and let cool. Top evenly with the caponata and serve.

MAKES ABOUT 30 SLICES

GREEN CHILI CORN CAKES WITH CAVIAR

The slight nip of mild green chilies complements the sweetness of the cornmeal in these delicate little cakes, paired with salty dollops of caviar. You can mix the batter, cook the pancakes and garnish them in a matter of minutes. Replace the caviar with minced tomato or bell pepper for a vegetarian version. Highlight the trio of tastes with a good champagne. (photograph page 42)

1 cup (8 fl oz/250 ml) milk

1 egg

2 tablespoons melted butter

$^{1}/_{2}$ cup (4 oz/125 g) minced canned or roasted and peeled fresh mild green chilies

$^{1}/_{2}$ cup (2$^{1}/_{2}$ oz/75 g) all-purpose (plain) flour

$^{1}/_{2}$ cup (2$^{1}/_{2}$ oz/75 g) cornmeal

2 teaspoons baking powder

$^{1}/_{2}$ teaspoon salt

$^{1}/_{2}$ teaspoon ground cumin

$^{1}/_{2}$ cup (4 fl oz/125 ml) crème fraîche or sour cream

2 oz (60 g) sturgeon caviar or other caviar

lime wedges for garnish

In a medium bowl, whisk together the milk, egg, melted butter and green chilies. Gradually blend in the flour, cornmeal, baking powder, salt and cumin, mixing thoroughly between additions to avoid lumps.

Cook the corn cakes by dropping the batter in $^{1}/_{8}$-cup (1-oz/30 g) portions onto a lightly buttered nonstick pan or griddle over medium-high heat. Turn carefully with a spatula when small bubbles come to the surface and the bottoms are golden brown, 3–5 minutes. Cook until browned on the second side, about $^{1}/_{2}$–1 minute. Serve topped with crème fraîche or sour cream and a dollop of caviar. Garnish with the lime wedges.

MAKES 26–28 CAKES

*Left to right: Creamy Chicken Canapés, Crab and Roasted Pepper Nachos
(recipe page 60), Corn Nachos (recipe page 61)*

1 whole boneless chicken breast, skinned, poached and shredded

8 oz (250 g) cream cheese at room temperature

2 jalapeño chilies, seeded and minced

3 tablespoons minced red (Spanish) onion

2 cloves garlic, minced

1 teaspoon cumin seed, crushed to a coarse powder

1 teaspoon chili powder

1¹/₂ cups (6 oz/185 g) grated Monterey Jack cheese

salt and freshly ground pepper

about 100 tortilla chips

CREAMY CHICKEN CANAPÉS

You could call these tostaditas, like the recipe on page 65, though they do bear a demure resemblance to classic cocktail hors d'oeuvres. There is nothing tame, however, about the spicy flavor they get from jalapeño chilies. When using these familiar chilies, it's a good idea to add only a portion of the amount called for, then taste for "heat" before adding more. Cooked shrimp may be substituted for the chicken. The topping, which may be made a day ahead, is also delicious on toast rounds.

In a medium bowl, cream together all the ingredients except the tortilla chips until well blended. The mixture can be stored in a covered container in the refrigerator for 1–2 days until needed. Bring to room temperature so that it is spreadable.

Preheat a broiler (griller). Evenly spread each chip with a generous amount of the chicken mixture. Arrange the chips on a baking sheet and broil (grill) about 3 in (7.5 cm) away from the heat until puffed and golden.

MAKES ABOUT 100 CANAPÉS

2 tablespoons unsalted butter

$^1/_2$ cup (2$^1/_2$ oz/75 g) minced onion

1 cup (8 fl oz/250 ml) heavy
(double) cream

$^1/_3$ cup (3 oz/90 g) cream cheese
at room temperature, cut
into pieces

$^1/_4$ cup (1 oz/30 g) grated asadero,
provolone or mozzarella cheese

$^1/_8$ teaspoon cayenne pepper

salt and freshly ground white
pepper

8 oz (250 g) fresh or thawed and
well-drained frozen crabmeat

1 red bell pepper (capsicum),
roasted, peeled, seeded and diced

2 Anaheim chilies, roasted, peeled,
seeded and diced

about 36 tortilla chips

CRAB AND ROASTED PEPPER NACHOS

The traditional Southwestern cocktail snack takes a decidedly nouvelle turn with a rich topping combining crabmeat, sweet and hot peppers, cream cheese and asadero, a Mexican cheese that resembles provolone in flavor and mozzarella in texture. Try the mixture on toasted baguette slices or enfolded in a crisped flour tortilla to make an upscale quesadilla.

In a medium sauté pan over medium-high heat, melt the butter. Add the onion and sauté until slightly softened, about 2 minutes. Add the cream, bring to a boil and cook, stirring occasionally, until the cream is reduced by half. Add the cream cheese and stir until blended. Stir in the asadero, provolone or mozzarella cheese, cayenne and salt and pepper to taste. Fold in the crabmeat, bell pepper and chilies. The mixture can be stored in a covered container in the refrigerator for 1–2 days. Bring to room temperature so that it is spreadable.

Preheat a broiler (griller). Spread each tortilla chip with about 1 tablespoon of the crab mixture and place on a baking sheet. Broil (grill) about 3 in (7.5 cm) from the heat until the nachos are hot and bubbly, 2–3 minutes.

MAKES ABOUT 36 NACHOS

1 tablespoon vegetable oil

¹/₂ cup (2¹/₂ oz/75 g) minced red
   bell pepper (capsicum)

¹/₃ cup (1¹/₂ oz/45 g) minced red
   (Spanish) onion

³/₄ cup (4 oz/125 g) corn kernels

3 Anaheim chilies, roasted, peeled,
   seeded and diced

8 oz (250 g) cream cheese at room
   temperature

1 cup (8 oz/250 g) sour cream

2 teaspoons chili powder

2 teaspoons ground cumin

¹/₄ teaspoon cayenne pepper

salt and freshly ground pepper

about 72 white or yellow corn
   chips

1 tablespoon sliced pickled
   jalapeño chilies (optional)

❂ CORN NACHOS

A popular finger food throughout the American Southwest, nachos may be as simple as a few corn chips topped with melted cheese or as elaborate as a mound of chips crowned with chicken or beef, refried beans, roasted mild green and pickled jalapeño chilies, tomatoes, guacamole and sour cream. This vegetarian version features corn and red bell pepper. Spice it up, if you wish, with pickled jalapeño slices.

In a large sauté pan over medium-high heat, warm the olive oil. Sauté the bell pepper and red onion until soft, about 3 minutes. Add the corn and Anaheim chilies and cook 2 minutes. Set aside.

In a medium bowl, beat together the cream cheese and sour cream. Add the chili powder, cumin, cayenne and salt and pepper to taste. Fold the sautéed vegetables into the cheese–sour cream mixture. The mixture can be stored in a covered container in the refrigerator for 1–2 days. Bring to room temperature so that it is spreadable.

Preheat a broiler (griller). Spread about ¹/₂ tablespoon of the topping on each corn chip. Sprinkle with the pickled jalapeños, if desired. Place on a baking sheet and broil (grill) about 3 in (7.5 cm) from the heat until the cheese melts and the chips begin to brown, about 2–3 minutes.

MAKES ABOUT 72 NACHOS

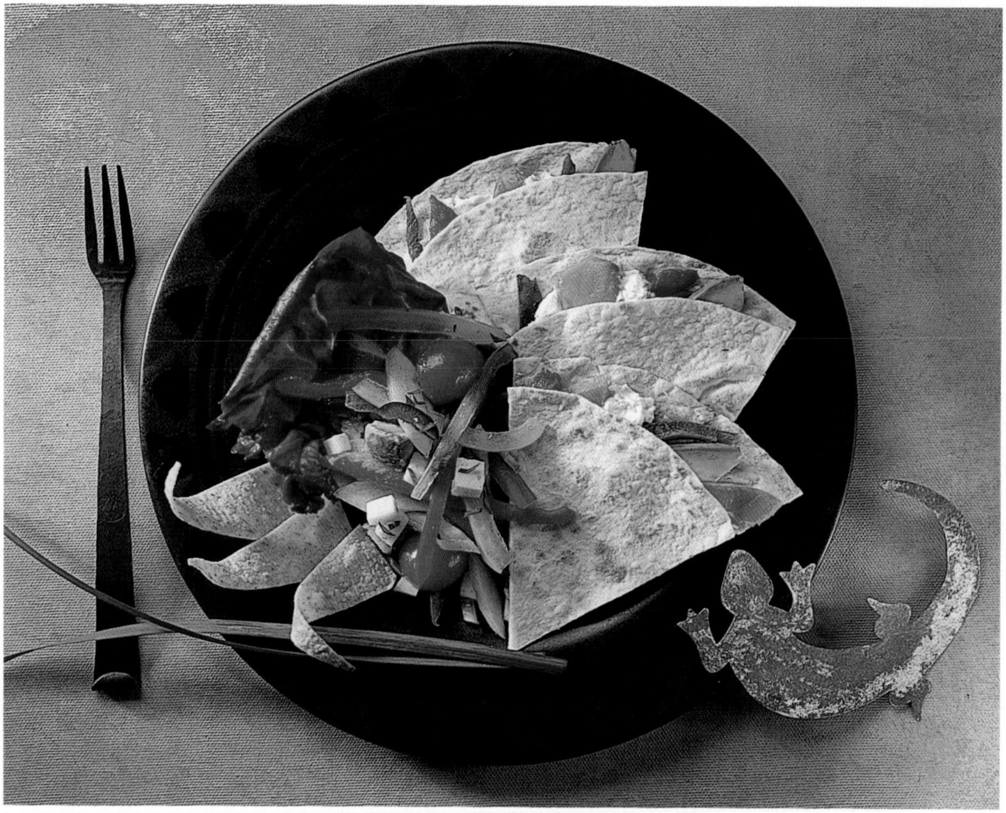

1/4 cup (2 oz/60 g) mild goat cheese

1/4 cup (2 oz/60 g) cream cheese
at room temperature

3 flour tortillas, 8 in (20 cm)
in diameter

1 poblano chili, roasted, peeled,
seeded, and cut into strips

1 red bell pepper (capsicum),
roasted, peeled, seeded, and cut
into strips

1 avocado, peeled, pitted and cut
into thin slices

1/4 cup (2 oz/60 g) minced shallots

2 oz (60 g) cold-smoked salmon,
cut into strips

SMOKED SALMON QUESADILLAS

The grilled cheese sandwiches of Mexico, quesadillas are, at their most basic, cheese melted inside a folded tortilla that is crisped in a frying pan, on a grill or under a broiler, then cut into wedges for eating by hand. In this robust version, the filling combination is quintessential modern Southwest cuisine, pairing cream and goat cheeses with roasted chilies and salmon.

In a small bowl, mix together the goat cheese and cream cheese until smooth and creamy. Spread one-third of the mixture over half of each flour tortilla.

Divide the poblano and red bell pepper strips evenly among the cheese-covered tortilla halves. Layer the avocado slices over the pepper strips and top with the shallots. Divide the salmon evenly among the tortilla halves. Fold the tortillas over, pressing to seal.

Heat a large, nonstick skillet over medium-high heat. Toast the tortillas until the cheese melts and they are brown on one side. Turn over and brown on the other side. Cut each quesadilla into 4 wedges. Serve immediately.

MAKES 12 QUESADILLAS

6 tablespoons (3 oz/90 g) unsalted butter at room temperature

2 oz (60 g) cream cheese at room temperature

$1/2$ cup ($2^1/2$ oz/75 g) yellow cornmeal

1 cup (5 oz/155 g) unbleached all-purpose (plain) flour

salt and freshly ground pepper

5 ripe plum (Roma) tomatoes, diced

$1/3$ cup ($1^1/2$ oz/45 g) minced red (Spanish) onion

1 red bell pepper (capsicum), seeded and diced

2 jalapeño chilies, seeded and minced

2 tablespoons fresh lemon juice

1 tablespoon fresh lime juice

$1/2$ cup (3 oz/90 g) cooked corn kernels

2 tablespoons minced fresh cilantro (fresh coriander)

CORN CUPS WITH TOMATO-CORN SALSA

Miniature muffin tins produce baked cornmeal cups just the right size for popping into your mouth. Try them as containers for other favorite salsas or fillings, including guacamole. (photograph pages 46–47)

Preheat an oven to 350°F (180°C). To make the pastry, in a medium bowl, cream together the butter and cream cheese. Sift the cornmeal, flour and salt to taste into a small bowl. Gradually stir the dry mixture into the butter-cheese mixture until all of it is incorporated. Turn the dough onto a lightly floured work surface and knead briefly. Divide it into 1-in (2.5-cm) balls. Place each ball into a miniature muffin mold, pressing down in the center to fill the mold and form a cup. Bake until light brown and cooked through, about 20 minutes. Remove from the oven and let cool. Remove the corn cups from the molds.

To make the salsa, in a small bowl, stir together the tomatoes, onion, bell pepper, chilies, lemon and lime juice, corn, cilantro and salt and pepper to taste. Fill the corn cups with the salsa and serve immediately. The corn cups can be stored in an airtight container at room temperature for 2–3 days. The salsa can be kept in a covered container in the refrigerator for up to 4 days.

MAKES 30 CORN CUPS

CHICKEN, CHILI AND AVOCADO TOSTADITAS

2 tablespoons olive oil

2 tablespoons butter

1 onion, halved and thinly sliced
  lengthwise

3 cloves garlic, minced

1 tomato, diced

2 tablespoons fresh lime juice

salt

1 whole boneless chicken breast,
  skinned and diced

1 jalapeño chili, roasted, peeled,
  seeded and cut into strips

1 red bell pepper (capsicum),
  roasted, peeled, seeded and cut
  into strips

1 Anaheim chili, roasted, peeled,
  seeded and cut into strips

1/4 cup (1/3 oz/10 g) minced fresh
  cilantro (fresh coriander)

1 avocado, peeled, pitted and diced

1 cup (4 oz/125 g) grated queso
  fresco or Monterey Jack cheese

1/2 cup (2 1/2 oz/75 g) crumbled
  cotija, feta or goat cheese

36 tortilla chips

Crisp corn tortilla chips are ideal platforms for a flavorful topping of chicken, roasted chilies and avocado. You can omit the chicken and increase the vegetables for a vegetarian version. The topping also makes a delicious cheese crisp: broil a flour tortilla on one side, flip it, spread the chicken mixture on the unbrowned side, sprinkle with cheese and broil until melted; then cut into wedges. Queso Fresco is a fresh cheese that is lower in fat, sodium and cholesterol than Monterey Jack or Cheddar cheese. Cotija is a hard, dry, full-flavored aged cheese. (photograph pages 46–47)

In a large, heavy skillet over medium heat, warm the olive oil and butter. Add the onion and cook until slightly softened, about 2 minutes. Add the garlic, tomato, lime juice and salt to taste. Cook, stirring, until the onion is translucent, about 5 minutes. Add the chicken and continue cooking until it is just opaque (do not overcook). Add the chili and pepper strips, cilantro and avocado. Remove from the heat.

Preheat a broiler (griller). Combine the cheeses in a small bowl. Spoon 1 tablespoon of the chicken mixture on each chip and top with grated cheese. Place the tortilla chips on a baking sheet. Broil (grill) about 3 in (7.5 cm) from the heat until the cheeses just begin to melt. Transfer to a serving platter and serve immediately.

MAKES 36 TOSTADITAS

2 eggs

1 cup (8 fl oz/250 ml) milk

¹/₄ teaspoon dried oregano leaves, crumbled

¹/₂ teaspoon fresh rosemary leaves, crushed

1 teaspoon salt

1¹/₄ cups (6¹/₂ oz/200 g) all-purpose (plain) flour

3 oz (90 g) spicy green olives, coarsely chopped

3 oz (90 g) spicy black olives, coarsely chopped

¹/₂ teaspoon crushed red pepper flakes (optional)

¹/₂ cup (4 fl oz/125 ml) olive oil

DESERT FLAT BREAD

The rough-and-ready character of pioneer cooking shines through in this old Texas favorite, which may be cut into wedges like a pizza and passed around to enjoy with a cold brew or, perhaps, sangria. You can vary the herbs to suit your taste, or replace the olives with chopped pickled jalapeños or roasted fresh chilies, or crumble goat cheese over the top before baking.

Preheat an oven to 350°F (180°C). Generously oil a cast-iron frying pan or baking dish 12 in (30 cm) in diameter.

In a medium bowl, whisk together the eggs and milk. Add the oregano, rosemary, salt and flour and stir to form a smooth batter. Stir in the green and black olives, pepper flakes (if using) and olive oil. Pour into the prepared pan. Bake until lightly browned, 25–35 minutes. Remove from the oven, cut into wedges and serve hot or at room temperature.

MAKES 8–10 WEDGES

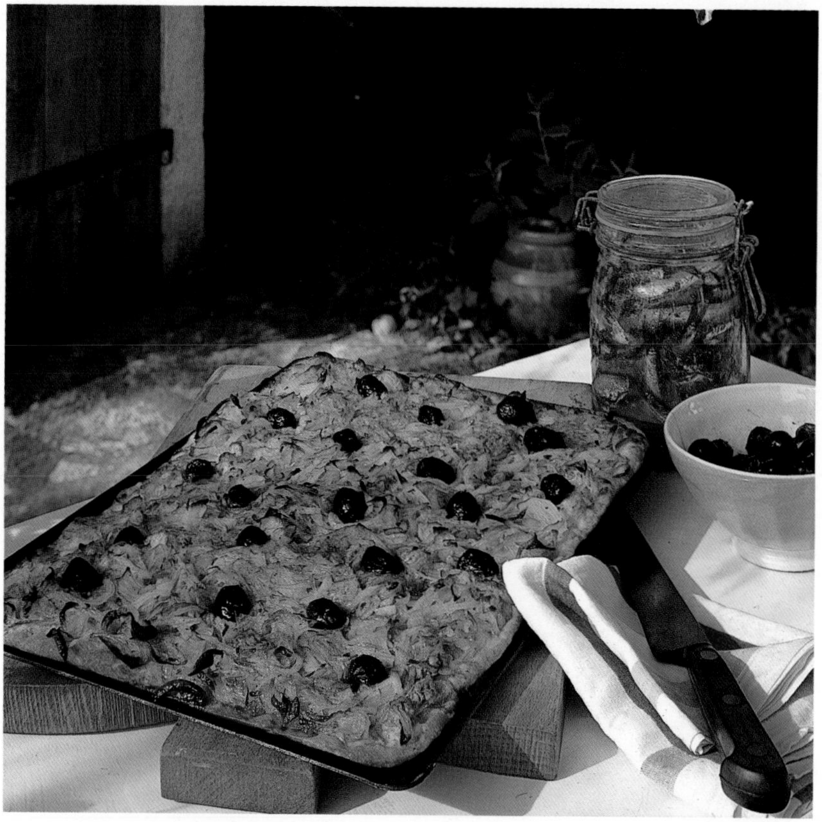

ANCHOVY AND ONION TART

The Provençale pissaladière *is generally considered to be the ancestor of the pizza. Instead of using the traditional yeast-leavened bread dough, this version is more quickly and easily assembled with a simple tartlike pastry enriched with olive oil. Serve with a young red wine or chilled beer.*

2 cups (10 oz/315 g) all-purpose (plain) flour

large pinch of salt

1 egg

¹/₄ cup (2 fl oz/60 ml) extra-virgin olive oil

¹/₄ cup (2 fl oz/60 ml) lukewarm water

¹/₃ cup (3 fl oz/80 ml) extra-virgin olive oil

10–12 white onions, thinly sliced

3 or 4 cloves garlic

salt and freshly ground pepper

1 bay leaf

1 fresh thyme sprig

16 anchovy fillets, mashed

³/₄ cup (4 oz/125 g) pitted black olives

To prepare the dough, combine the flour and pinch of salt in a medium bowl and mix with a fork. Add the egg, the ¹/₄ cup (2 fl oz/60 ml) olive oil and the water. Mix first with the fork, then knead in the bowl until you have a soft, consistent dough. Form into a ball and leave in the bowl. Cover with a towel and let stand at room temperature for about 1 hour.

To make the filling, warm half of the ¹/₃ cup (3 fl oz/80 ml) olive oil in a flameproof earthenware casserole or a heavy sauté pan over very low heat. Add the onions, garlic, salt to taste, bay leaf and thyme. Cover and cook over the lowest possible heat for about 1 hour, stirring occasionally. The onions must not color. If the heat is low enough, they will be white and as soft as a purée after 1 hour of cooking. Remove from the heat and discard the bay leaf and thyme sprig. Stir in the anchovies.

Preheat an oven to 350°F (180°C). Lightly oil a large baking sheet. Place the dough on a floured work surface. Flatten the dough, then sprinkle it with more flour. Roll out thinly to the approximate size of the baking sheet. Press the pastry gently onto the bottom and sides of the sheet. Roll the edges under to form a rim and crimp the edges. Prick the surface of the pastry with the tines of a fork, then spread the onion mixture over the pastry. Distribute the olives evenly over the onion mixture, half burying them. Brush the rim of the pastry with a little of the remaining olive oil, then sprinkle a bit more over the surface of the onions.

Bake until the pastry rim is golden and crisp, 30 minutes. Remove from the oven and grind with pepper. Cut into squares and arrange on a platter.

MAKES ABOUT 30 SQUARES

FROM BROCHETTES TO NUTS

As the recipes that follow vividly illustrate, anything you can pop in your mouth classifies as finger food. Sticks or florets of raw or parboiled vegetables with a fragrant dressing for dipping; fresh oysters on the half shell; crisply deep-fried potato chips, calamari, Asian shrimp puffs or all-American onion rings; skewers of grilled chicken or pork—all pique the appetite and encourage easy eating by hand.

The very simplicity of such dishes invites inventive presentation. You might want to set up a small barbecue or hibachi on a patio or terrace for guests to grill their own brochettes. Or you might fill a large punch bowl with crushed ice on which to array oysters or chilled cooked prawns. Just have at hand containers where guests can discreetly dispose of skewers or shells.

Some recipes, particularly the fried and grilled dishes, are best reserved for times when you are entertaining just a few people, or when you have help in the kitchen to ensure a steady stream of freshly cooked, hot hors d'oeuvres for guests. Others, including such classic cocktail snacks as roasted nuts and spiced olives, not only require advance preparation but store well, making them models of convenience for any occasion.

Spiced Olives (recipe page 90)

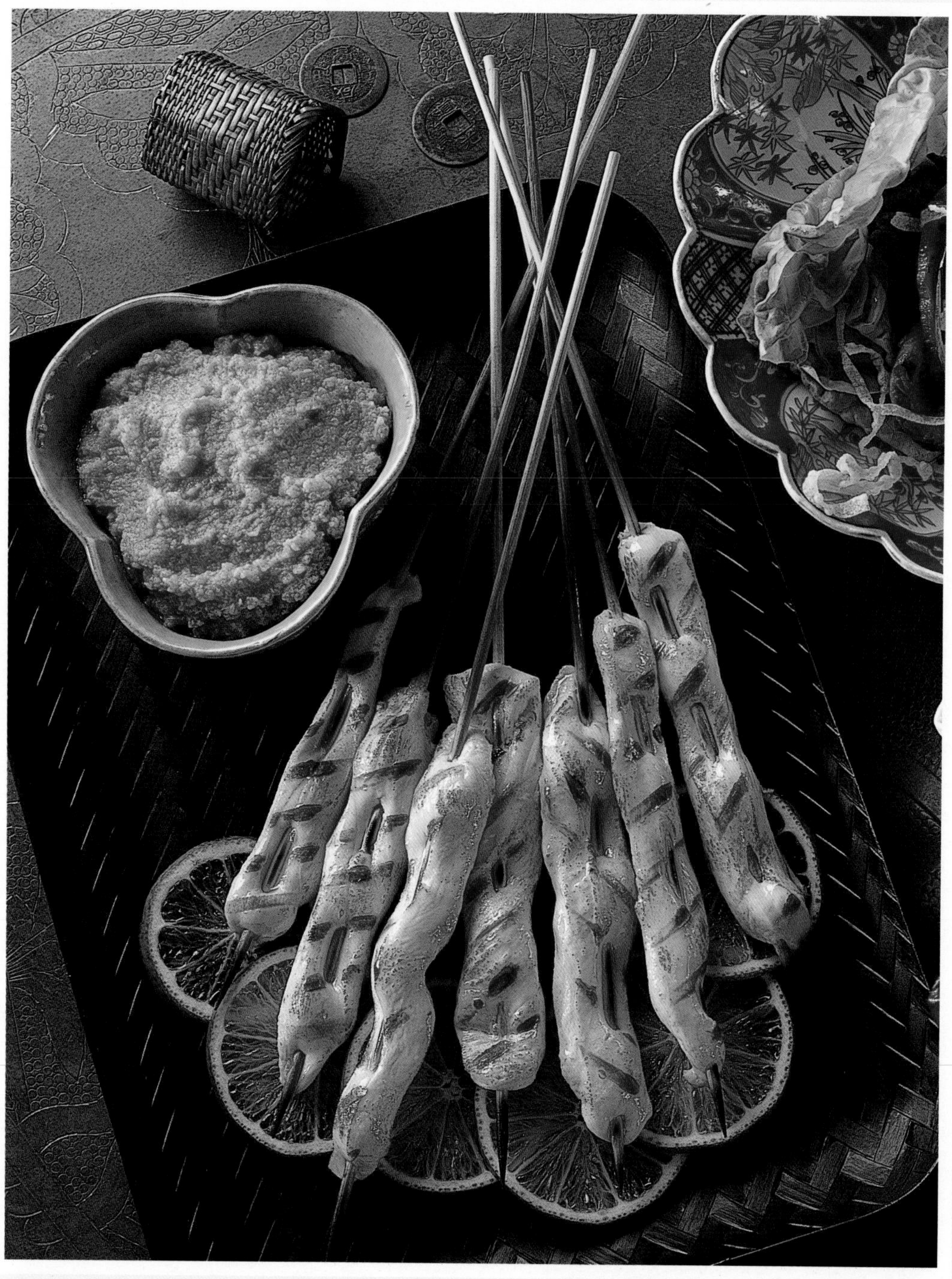

CHICKEN SLIVERS WITH CHIPOTLE-PEANUT SAUCE

1 tablespoon olive oil

3 cloves garlic, chopped

1 onion, coarsely chopped

2 tomatoes, chopped

4 chipotle chilies in adobo

$1/2$ cup (3 oz/90 g) unsalted
  peanuts or pumpkin seeds

$1/2$ cup (4 fl oz/125 ml) chicken
  stock

salt

4 boneless, skinless chicken
  breast halves

lime wedges for garnish

Inspired by the Indonesian brochettes known as satay, these tender strips of chicken breast are nibbled right off the skewers on which they are quickly grilled. Chipotle chilies—the term for smoked jalapeños—replace the traditional Asian chilies in the dipping sauce. The recipe also works well with thin strips of beef fillet or pork tenderloin.

Preheat a broiler (griller). Soak 8 bamboo skewers in water to cover for 20–30 minutes.

To make the sauce, warm the oil in a medium sauté pan over medium heat. Add the garlic and onion and sauté until just softened, 2–3 minutes. Transfer the onion mixture to a blender or a food processor fitted with the metal blade. Add the tomatoes, chilies, peanuts or pumpkin seeds and stock. Purée until smooth. Return to the pan and simmer for 5 minutes to blend the flavors. Season to taste with salt. Remove from the heat and set aside.

To prepare the chicken, slice the breast halves into long, thin strips. Drain the skewers and thread the chicken strips onto them. Broil (grill), turning once, until the chicken is opaque throughout when cut into with a knife, about 2 minutes on each side.

Place the skewers on a warmed platter and garnish with the lime wedges. Serve the sauce in a small bowl alongside.

MAKES 8 SKEWERS

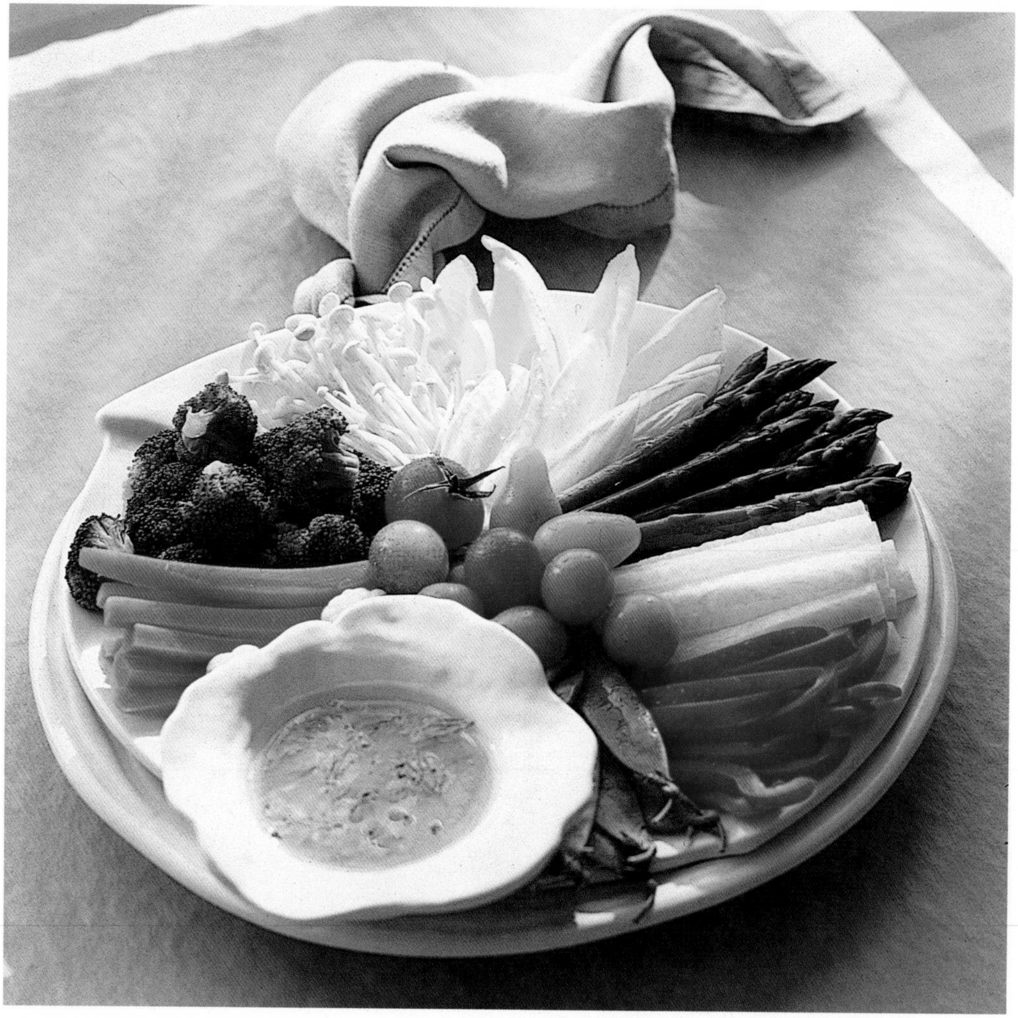

1/2 cup (4 fl oz/125 ml) vegetable
   stock

1/4 cup (2 fl oz/60 ml) fresh
   lemon juice

1/4 cup (2 fl oz/60 ml) white
   wine vinegar

1/2 cup (4 fl oz/125 ml) extra-virgin
   olive oil

2 teaspoons finely grated
   lemon zest

2 teaspoons fresh chopped dill

freshly ground pepper

1/4 lb (125 g) broccoli florets,
   blanched

1/4 lb (125 g) green beans, blanched

1/4 lb (125 g) snow peas
   (mangetouts)

1/4 lb (125 g) asparagus spears,
   trimmed to 3-in (7.5-cm) lengths
   and blanched

2 cups (12 oz/375 g) red or yellow
   cherry tomatoes

2 red or yellow bell peppers
   (capsicums), seeded and cut into
   narrow strips

3 heads Belgian endive (witloof),
   leaves separated

❷ CRUDITÉS WITH LEMON-DILL VINAIGRETTE

As healthy as finger food could possibly get, crudités put fresh seasonal vegetables into the spotlight. Cut them when necessary into bite-sized pieces and blanch those that gain finer flavor from brief exposure to boiling water. Let the selection available in your local market guide you into assembling your own array, choosing with an eye toward a variety of tastes, textures, colors and shapes. Substitute whatever dressing you like.

To make the vinaigrette, in a small saucepan over medium heat, cook the vegetable stock until it is reduced by half. Set aside to cool. In a medium bowl, combine the stock, lemon juice and vinegar. Slowly drizzle in the olive oil, whisking constantly. Stir in the lemon zest and dill. Season with pepper to taste and transfer to a small serving bowl.

Arrange all the vegetables on a platter. Accompany with the vinaigrette.

SERVES 10–12

1/2 cup (2 oz/60 g) finely grated
   Parmesan cheese

3/4 cup (4 oz/125 g) plain
   (all-purpose) flour

1/2 teaspoon salt

1/2 teaspoon baking powder

1/8 teaspoon cayenne pepper

1/2 cup (4 oz/125 g) unsalted
   butter, at room temperature,
   cut into small bits

✿ PARMESAN CHEESE BISCUITS

Light and flavorful, these quickly prepared biscuits offer the perfect complement to a glass of champagne. You can make them up to 3 days in advance, storing them at room temperature in an airtight container. For the best flavor, be sure to buy a block of imported Italian Parmesan, grating it freshly yourself. (photograph page 38)

Preheat an oven to 350°F (180°C). Butter and flour 2 baking sheets.

In a large bowl, stir together the cheese, flour, salt, baking powder and cayenne. Add the butter and, using 2 knives or a pastry blender, work it into the dry ingredients until the mixture comes together in a rough mass. Shape the dough into a ball, wrap in plastic wrap and refrigerate for 30 minutes.

On a lightly floured surface, roll out the dough 1/3 in (9 mm) thick. Dip a biscuit cutter 2 in (5 cm) in diameter in flour and cut out rounds, dipping the cutter as needed to prevent sticking. Place the rounds 1 in (2.5 cm) apart on the prepared baking sheets. Prick each biscuit twice with a fork.

Bake until golden, 8–10 minutes. Transfer to wire racks to cool. Serve warm or at room temperature.

MAKES ABOUT 40 BISCUITS

❶ POTATO WEDGES WITH CHILI AÏOLI

4 russet or other frying potatoes

1½ teaspoons salt

vegetable oil for deep-frying

4 cloves garlic

1 fresh red chili

2 egg yolks

1 cup (8 fl oz/250 ml) extra-virgin olive oil

Frying these long, thick-cut potato wedges twice bestows incomparable crispness, and leaving their peels on adds an appealingly rustic quality. If you are leery of making mayonnaise from scratch, use a good-quality commercial brand, puréeing the garlic and chili in a miniature food processor or with a mortar and pestle before stirring it in. (photograph page 54)

Scrub the potatoes but do not peel. Place in a medium saucepan with water to cover barely. Add 1 teaspoon of the salt and bring to a boil. Reduce the heat to medium and simmer, uncovered, until the potatoes are just tender, 8 minutes or longer, depending on their size. Drain and let cool completely.

In a large, heavy pan, pour in the vegetable oil to a depth of 2 in (5 cm). Heat the oil slowly.

To make the aïoli, in a food processor fitted with the metal blade or in a blender, place the garlic and chili and process to chop. Add the egg yolks and the remaining ½ teaspoon salt and process until thick. With the motor running, slowly add half of the olive oil, drop by drop, until incorporated. Then add the remaining oil in a thin, steady stream and process until thickened. Spoon into a small serving bowl and set aside.

To cook the potatoes, cut them into eighths. Test the oil temperature by dropping a small piece of bread into it. If it immediately rises to the surface, the oil is ready. Working in batches, slip the potatoes into the oil and fry until golden, about 8 minutes. Transfer to paper towels to drain.

When all the potatoes have been fried, reheat the oil and recook them, again in batches, until crisp, about 3 minutes. Transfer them to paper towels to drain. Serve piping hot, accompanied with the aïoli.

MAKES 32 WEDGES

OYSTERS WITH PICKLED GINGER, DAIKON AND LIME

Fresh oysters are usually enjoyed with a mere squeeze of lemon or a dash of to-mato-horseradish cocktail sauce—which is why this Asian-style treatment, with the vibrant flavors of ginger, daikon and lime, is such a refreshing change of pace. To make the recipe all the easier, ask your fishmonger to shuck the oysters for you, packing them in their half shells nestled in a bed of crushed ice.

Scrub the oysters, open them and discard the top shells. Loosen the oyster meats from the bottom shells and leave them in the shells.

Arrange the oysters on a platter. Scatter the ginger and daikon evenly over the tops. Place a cilantro leaf on each oyster. Garnish the platter with lime halves. Refrigerate until well chilled, then serve.

MAKES 18 OYSTERS

18 medium oysters

$^1/_4$ cup (1 oz/30 g) pickled ginger slices, cut into fine julienne

$^1/_2$ cup (2$^1/_2$ oz/75 g) daikon, cut into fine julienne

18 fresh cilantro (fresh coriander) leaves

2 limes, halved, for garnish

SHRIMP PUFFS WITH SESAME SEEDS

Far East meets Southwest in these golden fried shrimp with a sweet-hot dipping sauce. Although the recipe calls for black sesame seeds, white sesame seeds may replace them.

8 large shrimp (prawns)

2 teaspoons dry sherry

3 tablespoons Dijon-style mustard

$^{1}/_{4}$ cup (2 fl oz/60 ml) heavy (double) cream

1 tablespoon black sesame seeds, toasted

1 cup (5 oz/155 g) all-purpose (plain) flour

1 teaspoon baking powder

1 tablespoon black sesame seeds

1 cup (8 fl oz/250 ml) water

peanut oil for deep-frying

2 tablespoons cornstarch (cornflour)

Peel, devein and butterfly the shrimp. Place in a small bowl and sprinkle with the sherry. Let stand 10 minutes. To make the sauce, in a small bowl, combine the mustard, cream and sesame seeds and mix well. Set aside.

To prepare the shrimp, in a medium bowl, stir together the flour, baking powder, sesame seeds and water until smooth. Pour the peanut oil into a deep, heavy skillet to a depth of $1^{1}/_{2}$ in (4 cm). Heat to 360°F (182°C). Spread the cornstarch on a plate. Dip each shrimp first into the cornstarch, coating both sides and shaking off any excess, and then into the batter. Slip the shrimp into the oil and deep-fry until lightly browned and cooked through, 2–3 minutes. Transfer to paper towels to drain briefly.

Serve the shrimp piping hot with the mustard sauce on the side.

MAKES 8 SHRIMP PUFFS

🍂 ITALIAN BREAD DIPPED IN OIL AND SAGE

Think of this as a minimalist Italian version of fondue, with strips of a peasant loaf immersed by each guest in a hot, fragrant olive oil and herb bath until golden brown. Set the pot of oil on a hot plate in the middle of the buffet table, so that the oil stays very hot. Place long-handled forks and a basket of bread strips close by for spearing and dipping.

1 cup (8 fl oz/250 ml) extra-virgin olive oil

10 large fresh sage leaves

1 clove garlic

6 slices coarse country bread, cut into finger-sized strips

salt

Pour the olive oil into a pot, preferably made of flameproof earthenware, and warm over moderate heat to 325°F (165°C). Add the sage leaves and garlic and cook until the leaves are crisp, about 1 minute, or until the temperature reaches 350°F (180°C).

Place the pot on a hot plate. Provide guests with long-handled forks. Instruct them to spear the bread and immerse it in the hot oil until golden, about 3 minutes. When the bread is lifted from the oil, any excess oil can be allowed to drip back into the pot. Guests may season the bread with salt to taste.

SERVES 6–8

2 lb (1 kg) pork, cut into 1-in
   (2.5-cm) cubes

$^{1}/_{2}$ cup (4 fl oz/125 ml) olive oil

1 tablespoon paprika

2 tablespoons ground cumin

1 teaspoon chopped fresh thyme

2 teaspoons cayenne pepper

1 teaspoon chopped fresh oregano

2 teaspoons minced garlic

SPANISH PORK BROCHETTES

You'll find spicy pork morsels such as these all over Spain in the tapas bars, where people go to enjoy a glass of sherry or wine with a wide assortment of finger foods. The Spanish name for the dish, pincho moruno, *which literally means "Moorish or Arabic mouthfuls," gives away its origin. In Arab countries, however, lamb is the meat of choice, and you may substitute it for the pork.*

Place the meat in a nonreactive container. In a small sauté pan over low heat, warm the oil and add all the remaining ingredients. Let cool and pour over the meat to coat evenly. Cover and refrigerate overnight.

Bring the meat to room temperature. Soak 8 bamboo skewers in water for 20–30 minutes. Preheat a broiler (griller). Thread the meat onto the skewers and broil (grill), turning once, until done to taste, about 4 minutes per side for medium-rare. Transfer to a warmed platter and serve.

MAKES 8 BROCHETTES

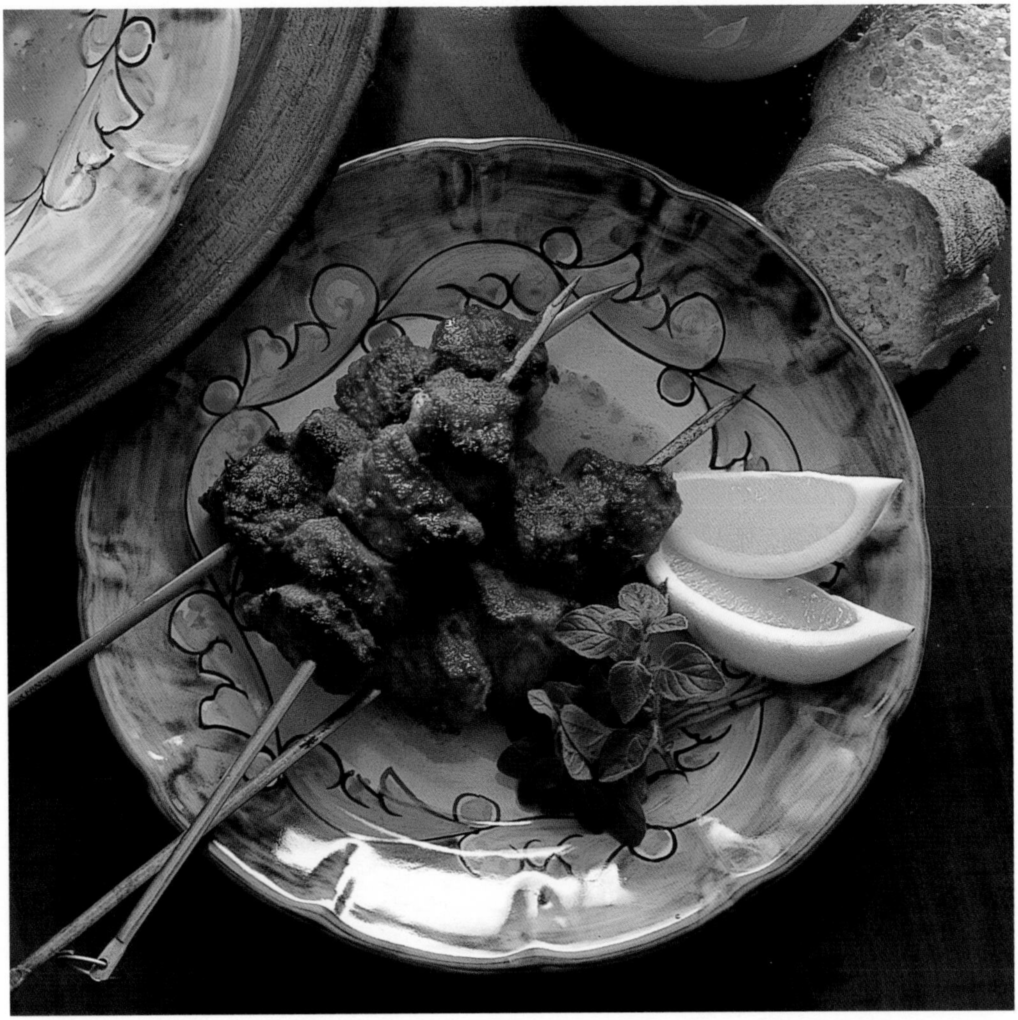

Top to bottom: Toasted Spicy Nuts, Beer-Battered Onion Rings (recipe page 86)

1 lb (500 g) walnut halves
  and pieces

1 lb (500 g) hazelnuts

$^1/_3$ cup (3 fl oz/80 ml) honey

$1^1/_2$ teaspoons ground ginger

$1^1/_2$ teaspoons ground coriander

$^1/_2$ teaspoon cayenne pepper

1 tablespoon kosher salt

❼ TOASTED SPICY NUTS

A far cry from packaged mixed nuts, these have just enough zip to keep you coming back for more and to contrast delightfully with cold beer or cocktails. Roast them in big batches for the holiday season; an airtight container will keep them crisp and crunchy for several weeks.

Preheat an oven to 375°F (190°C). Place the walnuts and hazelnuts in a large roasting pan and toast in the oven for 5 minutes, stirring once or twice. While the nuts are toasting, heat all the remaining ingredients except the salt in a small saucepan over medium heat. Bring the mixture to a low boil and remove from the heat.

Remove the nuts from the oven, leaving the oven on. Pour the honey mixture over the toasted nuts and stir thoroughly to coat all the nuts evenly. Return the nuts to the oven and toast for 15–20 minutes more, stirring once or twice. Break a few of the nuts in half to see if they are golden brown inside. When they have reached this stage, remove the nuts from the oven and sprinkle the kosher salt evenly over them. To prevent the nuts from sticking together, stir them every 5 minutes for the first 15 minutes, then every 10 minutes until they are completely cool.

MAKES 2 LB (1 KG) NUTS

🌑 BEER-BATTERED ONION RINGS

Yeasty beer adds lightness and tang to the batter for this classic finger food. Choose one of the scores of microbrewery beers being produced today, and be sure to have extra on hand to sip alongside. Sweet varieties of onion are the best choice for deep-frying. Look for Walla Walla onions from Washington State, Vidalias from Georgia or Mauis from Hawaii, or use red onions.

³/₄ cup (4 oz/125 g) all-purpose (plain) flour

³/₄ cup (3 oz/90 g) cornstarch (cornflour)

¹/₂ teaspoon baking soda (bicarbonate of soda)

1 tablespoon sifted powdered (icing) sugar

2 teaspoons salt

¹/₄ teaspoon ground white pepper

¹/₄ teaspoon paprika

¹/₄ teaspoon dried dill

¹/₄ teaspoon dried thyme

¹/₂ teaspoon grated lemon zest

¹/₂–³/₄ cup (4–6 fl oz/125–180 ml) hearty ale (dark beer)

¹/₂ cup (4 fl oz/125 ml) plus 1–2 tablespoons water, if needed

¹/₂ cup (2¹/₂ oz/75 g) all-purpose (plain) flour

¹/₂ teaspoon salt

2 large, symmetrical, mild white onions

vegetable oil for deep-frying

In a large bowl, mix together the ³/₄ cup (4 oz/125 g) flour, cornstarch, baking soda, powdered sugar, 2 teaspoons salt, white pepper, paprika, dill, thyme and lemon zest. Stir in the ale and ¹/₂ cup (4 fl oz/125 ml) of the water to make a light batter that will coat the onion rings, adding the 1–2 tablespoons of water as needed. The batter should have the same consistency as crêpe batter. Place the ¹/₂ cup (2¹/₂ oz/75 g) flour and ¹/₂ teaspoon salt in a clean paper sack. Cut the onions into slices ¹/₃ in (9 mm) thick and separate into rings. Add the rings to the sack and shake gently to dredge with the flour.

In a deep, heavy pan, pour the vegetable oil to a depth of 2–3 in (5–7.5 cm). Heat the oil to 350°–375°F (180°–190°C). When the oil has reached the correct temperature, a cube of bread dropped in the oil will brown in 1 minute. Dip the onion rings in the batter and fry in batches until golden, about 2 minutes. Drain on paper towels and serve immediately.

SERVES 6–8

GRILLED SHRIMP WRAPPED IN BACON AND BASIL

8 long, woody fresh rosemary
  sprigs

1$^{1}/_{2}$ teaspoons unsulfured
  light molasses

2 cups (16 fl oz/500 ml) bottled
  chili sauce

1 chipotle chili, soaked in hot
  water to soften, drained
  and diced

$^{1}/_{4}$ cup (2 oz/60 g) butter

1 tablespoon Worcestershire sauce

3 fresh serrano chilies, thinly
  sliced lengthwise and seeded

36–40 large shrimp (prawns),
  peeled, deveined and butterflied
  with tail section intact

36–40 large fresh basil leaves

$^{1}/_{2}$ lb (250 g) bacon

Spicy, sweet and smoky, these hot-from-the-grill shrimp are irresistible, especially when enjoyed with a chilled glass of white wine that has a hint of fruitiness to counteract the heat of the chilies. You can, of course, use metal or bamboo skewers in place of the rosemary sprigs.

Place the rosemary sprigs in water to cover for 2–3 hours. Preheat a broiler (griller).

To make the sauce, combine the molasses, chili sauce, chipotle chili, butter and Worcestershire sauce in a small saucepan and place over medium heat. Bring to a simmer, stirring to mix well. Remove the sauce from the heat and keep warm until serving.

To cook the shrimp, place a small sliver of serrano chili inside each shrimp, press closed and wrap first with a basil leaf and then with a piece of bacon. Drain the rosemary sprigs and thread the shrimp onto them. Broil (grill), turning twice and basting frequently with the warm sauce, until just cooked, 3–4 minutes.

Serve the shrimp immediately, accompanied by any remaining sauce in a small bowl on the side.

MAKES 8 SKEWERS

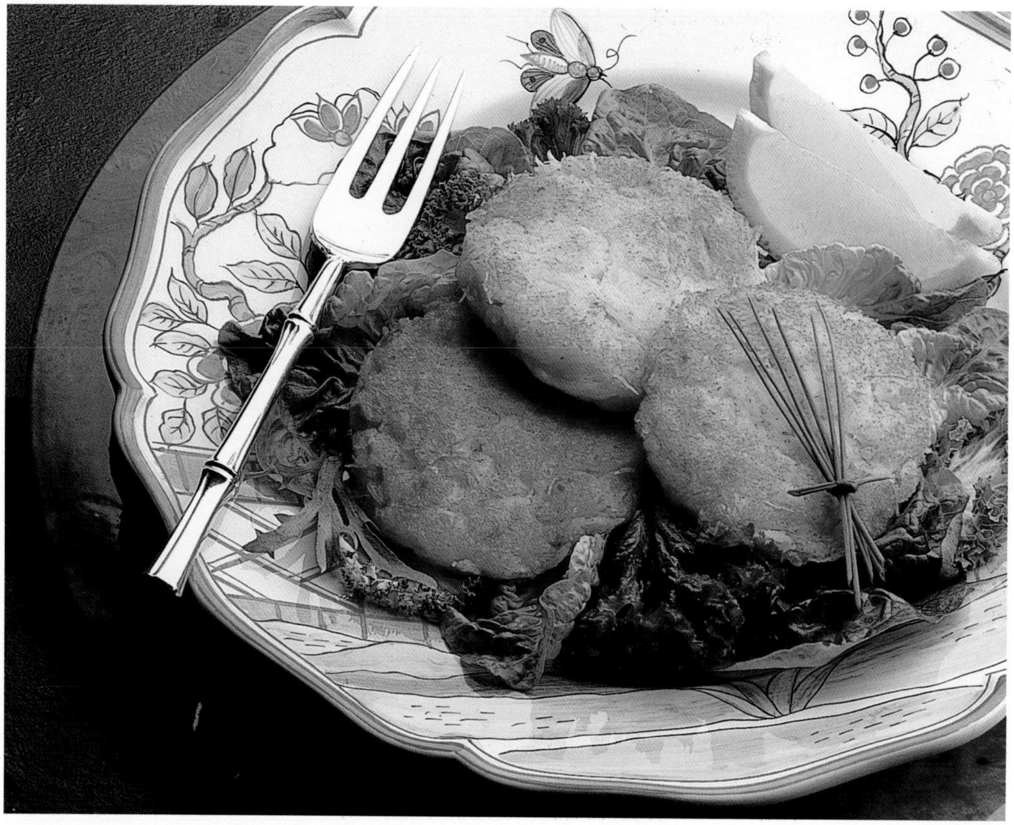

CRAB CAKES

2 cups (1 lb/500 g) crabmeat

1 tablespoon fresh lemon juice

2 cups (1 lb/500 g) warm mashed
  potatoes

4 egg yolks

1 tablespoon Dijon mustard

$^1/_8$ teaspoon cayenne pepper

1 teaspoon salt

freshly ground pepper

$^1/_3$ cup (3 fl oz/80 ml) olive oil or
  clarified butter

There are so many different ways to make crab cakes. This method, inspired by Stars, a restaurant in San Francisco, uses a base of mashed potatoes and egg yolks to yield lighter results than the more common crab cakes containing bread crumbs. If you'd like to make truly bite-sized crab cakes, use heaping tablespoons to shape the mixture, still carefully forming them into patties $^1/_2$ in (12 mm) thick.

Carefully pick over the crabmeat and remove any bits of shell or cartilage. Place in a small bowl, toss with the lemon juice and set aside.

In a large bowl, combine the potatoes, egg yolks, mustard, cayenne, salt and freshly ground pepper to taste. Fold in the crabmeat. Using generous $^1/_4$-cup (4-fl-oz/125-ml) portions, pat and shape the mixture into 12 patties, each about $^1/_2$ in (12 mm) thick.

Heat 3 tablespoons of the oil or butter in a large skillet over medium-high heat. Add as many crab cakes as you can without crowding them and cook until they are well browned, about 3 minutes on each side. Transfer to paper towels to drain. Fry the remaining cakes, adding more butter or oil as necessary. Serve immediately.

MAKES 12 CAKES

FOR GREEK OLIVES:

1 lb (500 g) Kalamata olives

4 tablespoons (¹/₃ oz/10 g) dried
   oregano

1 tablespoon dried rosemary

1 tablespoon dried thyme

2 strips orange zest, each about
   2 in (5 cm) long and ¹/₄ in
   (6 mm) wide

extra-virgin olive oil

FOR MOROCCAN OLIVES:

1 lb (500 g) black or green olives

6 tablespoons (¹/₂ oz/15 g)
   chopped fresh parsley

6 tablespoons (¹/₂ oz/15 g)
   chopped fresh cilantro
   (fresh coriander)

3 cloves garlic, chopped

1 teaspoon red pepper flakes or
   2 fresh chilies, slivered

¹/₂ teaspoon ground cumin

¹/₂ cup (4 fl oz/125 ml) extra-virgin
   olive oil

2 teaspoons fresh lemon juice or
   a few strips lemon zest

❂ SPICED OLIVES

A time-honored bar nibble, olives are natural companions to cocktails, most particularly dry martinis. This recipe begins with already-cured olives commonly available in markets and delicatessens, then elaborates upon them with your choice of two marinades that capture the authentic flavors of Greece and Morocco. The olives will keep well for 2–3 weeks in the refrigerator, only improving with flavor over time. (photograph pages 70–71)

Whether preparing Greek or Moroccan olives, drain the brine off the olives and rinse them well.

To make the Greek olives, dry the rinsed olives thoroughly, place in a medium bowl and combine with all the remaining ingredients, including olive oil to cover or coat.

To make the Moroccan olives, crack the rinsed olives, place in a medium bowl, add cold water to cover and let stand overnight. Drain well and combine with all the remaining ingredients.

Place the olives in a sterilized jar, cover tightly and refrigerate for at least 2 days to allow the flavors to blend.

MAKES 1 LB (500 G) OLIVES PER RECIPE

CHILLED SHRIMP WITH ANISE MAYONNAISE

1 shallot, coarsely chopped

2 tablespoons seasoned rice vinegar

2 tablespoons dry white wine

$^1/_2$ cup (2 oz/60 g) coarsely chopped fennel bulb

2 large egg yolks

1 tablespoon fresh lemon juice

1 tablespoon Pernod

1 teaspoon salt

$^3/_4$ cup (6 fl oz/180 ml) peanut (groundnut) oil

$^3/_4$ cup (6 fl oz/180 ml) mild olive oil

$^1/_4$ cup ($^1/_3$ oz/10 g) coarsely chopped fresh anise or fresh basil leaves

$1^1/_2$ cups (12 oz /375 ml) good-quality beer

4 cups (32 fl oz/1 l) water

6 cloves garlic, crushed

1 bay leaf

6 whole cloves

6 peppercorns

24 large shrimp (prawns)

One of summertime's great pleasures in coastal areas is to lazily consume a pile of chilled shrimp, peeling each by hand and pausing only to dip it in a sauce. This sauce, with its hint of licorice-scented anise, goes wonderfully with the succulent crustaceans. If you'd rather not make mayonnaise from scratch, blend the wine reduction, lemon juice, Pernod and herbs into a good commercial brand. (photograph page 53)

To make the mayonnaise, place the shallot, vinegar, white wine and fennel in a small saucepan. Simmer over medium-high heat until the shallot and fennel are tender and the liquid is reduced by half, about 10 minutes. In a blender or a food processor fitted with the metal blade, place the egg yolks, lemon juice, Pernod and salt. Process until the yolks are pale yellow, about 4 minutes. With the motor running, pour in the warm fennel mixture. Process until smooth, about 4 minutes. Add the peanut oil and olive oil in a slow, steady stream. The mixture will start to thicken as you reach the halfway point. Add the anise or basil leaves and pulse to finely chop the leaves. Refrigerate for 1 hour before serving to blend the flavors.

To prepare the shrimp, place the beer, water, garlic cloves, bay leaf, cloves and peppercorns in a large saucepan. Bring to a boil over medium-high heat. Let the mixture boil for 2 minutes, then add the shrimp and cover with a tight-fitting lid. Return the pot to a boil and cook for about 2 minutes, then remove from the heat and let the shrimp steep for 10 minutes.

Drain the shrimp and rinse them with cold water. Refrigerate in a covered container until ready to serve. If desired, the shrimp may be peeled before serving. Arrange on a chilled platter and accompany with anise mayonnaise.

MAKES 24 SHRIMP

FRIED CALAMARI WITH LEMON AÏOLI

How many lovers of fried calamari first got addicted when they inadvertently popped one of these golden circles into their mouths thinking it was an onion ring? Cooking the squid only just until it is barely golden, and no longer, ensures results that are tender, with a pleasant hint of chewiness, rather than rubbery. If you like, substitute your favorite cocktail sauce for the aïoli.

1 egg

1 egg yolk

3 cloves garlic

⅓ cup (3 fl oz/80 ml) fresh lemon juice

1 cup (8 fl oz/250 ml) extra-virgin olive oil

grated zest of 1 lemon

1 teaspoon salt plus salt to taste

1 cup (5 oz/155 g) all-purpose (plain) flour

1 tablespoon cornstarch (cornflour)

½ teaspoon ground white pepper

peanut (groundnut) oil for frying

2 lb (1 kg) small squid, cleaned and cut into ¼-in (6-mm) rings

lemon wedges for garnish

To make the aioli, place the egg, egg yolk, garlic cloves and lemon juice in a blender or in a food processor fitted with the metal blade. Process until smooth and creamy, about 3 minutes. With the motor running, gradually drizzle in the olive oil. After the aioli thickens, stir in the lemon zest and salt to taste. Cover and refrigerate for at least 1 hour before serving to blend the flavors.

To prepare the squid, combine the flour, cornstarch, 1 teaspoon salt and pepper in a medium bowl. In a deep, heavy skillet, pour peanut oil to a depth of 1 in (2.5 cm). Heat the oil to 350°F (180°C). When the oil is the correct temperature, a cube of bread dropped in the oil will brown in 1 minute. Dredge the squid rings, a few at a time, in the flour. Shake off the excess flour and sauté the squid until barely golden, about 2 minutes. Transfer the squid rings to paper towels to drain. Repeat until all the squid is cooked.

Arrange the squid on a warm platter, garnish with the lemon wedges and accompany with the aïoli.

SERVES 6–8

ACKNOWLEDGMENTS

Recipes and photographs in *Finger Food* first appeared in the following *Beautiful Cookbooks.*

RECIPES

Australia the Beautiful Cookbook, copyright © 1995, pages 37, 39, 49, 50, 51, 55, 56, 76, 77, 78. *California the Beautiful Cookbook,* copyright © 1991, pages 27, 44, 89. *Healthy Gourmet,* copyright © 1994, page 75. *Mediterranean the Beautiful Cookbook,* copyright © 1994, pages 28, 82, 90. *Pacific Northwest the Beautiful Cookbook,* copyright © 1993, pages 29, 31, 43, 53, 57, 85, 86, 91, 93. *Provence the Beautiful Cookbook,* copyright © 1993, page 69. *Southwest the Beautiful Cookbook,* copyright © 1994, pages 45, 59, 60, 61, 63, 64, 65. *Texas the Beautiful Cookbook,* copyright © 1995, pages 66, 73, 79, 87. *Thailand the Beautiful Cookbook,* copyright © 1992, pages 32, 35, 36. *Tuscany the Beautiful Cookbook,* copyright © 1992, pages 40, 41, 81.

PHOTOGRAPHY

E. J. Armstrong, copyright © 1993, pages 8, 30, 42, 52, 84, 92; copyright © 1994, pages 1, 14, 46–47, 58, 62; copyright © 1995, pages 67, 72, 79. **John Hay,** copyright © 1992, pages 13, 33, 34. **Peter Johnson,** copyright © 1992, pages 19, 40, 41, 51, 81; copyright © 1993, page 68; copyright © 1994, pages 50, 70–71, 83, 94; copyright © 1995, pages 2, 6–7, 38, 48–49, 54, 78. **Allan Rosenberg,** copyright © 1991, pages 24–25, 26, 88. **Philip Salaverry,** copyright © 1994, page 74.

INDEX

anchovies
  about 10
  Anchovy and Onion Tart *68*, 69
Avocado Tostaditas, Chicken, Chili
  and *46–47*, 65

beef
  Cocktail Pasties with Tomato
    Sauce *38*, 39
  Piroshki *26*, 27
Beer-Battered Onion Rings *84*, 86
bell peppers
  Crab and Roasted Pepper Nachos
    58, 60
  Red Pepper Puttanesca Canapés
    54, 55
  roasting 17
bread crumbs 16
breads
  about 11
  Italian Bread Dipped in Oil and
    Sage *80*, 81
Brochettes, Spanish Pork 82, *83*
Bruschetta, Vegetable 51, *51*
butter, clarified 16

Calamari, Fried, with Lemon Aïoli
  92, 93
capers 10
Caponata, Grilled Eggplant Topped
  with *54*, 56
Caviar, Green Chili Corn Cakes with
  42, 57
cheese
  about 11

Chicken, Chili and Avocado
  Tostaditas *46–47*, 65
Parmesan Cheese Biscuits *38*, 76
Smoked Salmon Quesadillas *62*, 63
chicken
  Chicken, Chili and Avocado
    Tostaditas *46–47*, 65
  Chicken Slivers with Chipotle-
    Peanut Sauce *72*, 73
  Creamy Chicken Canapés *58*, 59
chilies
  Chicken, Chili and Avocado
    Tostaditas *46–47*, 65
  Chicken Slivers with Chipotle-
    Peanut Sauce *72*, 73
  Cocktail-Size Chilies Rellenos
    45, *46–47*
  Crab and Roasted Pepper Nachos
    58, 60
  Green Chili Corn Cakes with
    Caviar *42*, 57
  handling 16
  Potato Wedges with Chili Aïoli
    54, 77
  roasting 17
Chilled Shrimp with Anise
  Mayonnaise *53*, 91
Cocktail Pasties with Tomato Sauce
  38, 39
Cocktail-Size Chilies Rellenos
  45, *46–47*
Corn Cups with Tomato-Corn Salsa
  46–47, 64
Corn Nachos *58*, 61

Crab and Roasted Pepper Nachos
  58, 60
Crab Cakes *88*, 89
Crab-Stuffed Mushrooms 29, *30*
crackers 11
Creamy Chicken Canapés *58*, 59
Crisp Fried Spring Rolls *34*, 36
Crudités with Lemon-Dill
  Vinaigrette *74*, 75

Desert Flat Bread 66, *67*
Dolmas *24–25*, 44
Dumplings, Rice Paper 32, *33*

Eggplant, Grilled, Topped with
  Caponata *54*, 56
Eggs, Stuffed, with Tarragon 40, *40*

fish. *See also* anchovies; salmon
  Piroshki *26*, 27
Fresh Thai Spring Rolls *34*, 35
Fried Calamari with Lemon Aioli
  92, 93
fruits 11

garlic, roasted 17
Green Chili Corn Cakes with Caviar
  42, 57
Grilled Eggplant Topped with
  Caponata *54*, 56
Grilled Shrimp Wrapped in Bacon
  and Basil 87

herbs 10–11

Italian Bread Dipped in Oil and Sage
  80, 81

menus 20–23

mushrooms
    Crab-Stuffed Mushrooms 29, *30*
    Wild Mushroom Filo Packets
        30, 31

Mussels, Stuffed, on the Half Shell
    41, *41*

nachos
    Corn Nachos *58*, 61
    Crab and Roasted Pepper Nachos
        58, 60

Nuts, Toasted Spicy *84*, 85

oils 9

olives
    about 10
    Desert Flat Bread 66, *67*
    pitting 17
    Spiced Olives *70–71*, 90

onions
    Anchovy and Onion Tart *68*, 69
    Beer-Battered Onion Rings *84*, 86

Oysters with Pickled Ginger, Daikon
    and Lime 78, *78*

Pancakes, Spinach, with Sour Cream
    and Salmon Roe *48*, 49

Parmesan Cheese Biscuits *38*, 76

pastries 11

Piroshki *26*, 27

pork
    Crisp Fried Spring Rolls *34*, 36
    Rice Paper Dumplings 32, *33*
    Spanish Pork Brochettes 82, *83*

Potato Wedges with Chili Aïoli *54*, 77

presentation 18–19

Quesadillas, Smoked Salmon *62*, 63

Red Pepper Puttanesca Canapés
    54, 55

Rice Paper Dumplings 32, *33*

Roasted Tomato Hearts *38*, 50

salmon
    Scallion Biscuits with Smoked
        Salmon Spread 52, *53*
    Shrimp-Filled Salmon Cones
        42, 43
    Smoked Salmon Lavash Rolls
        37, *48*
    Smoked Salmon Quesadillas *62*, 63

sausages
    Fresh Thai Spring Rolls *34*, 35
    Stuffed Mussels on the Half Shell
        41, *41*

Scallion Biscuits with Smoked
    Salmon Spread 52, *53*

shrimp
    Chilled Shrimp with Anise
        Mayonnaise *53*, 91
    Grilled Shrimp Wrapped in Bacon
        and Basil 87
    peeling and deveining 17
    Shrimp-Filled Salmon Cones
        42, 43
    Shrimp Puffs with Sesame Seeds
        79, *79*

Smoked Salmon Lavash Rolls 37, *48*

Smoked Salmon Quesadillas *62*, 63

Spanish Pork Brochettes 82, *83*

Spanokopita 28

specialty ingredients 12, 15

Spiced Olives 70–71, 90

spices 10–11

spinach
    Spanokopita 28
    Spinach Pancakes with Sour
        Cream and Salmon Roe 48, 49

spring rolls
    Crisp Fried Spring Rolls *34*, 36
    Fresh Thai Spring Rolls *34*, 35

stocks 9–10

Stuffed Eggs with Tarragon 40, *40*

Stuffed Mussels on the Half Shell
    41, *41*

Toasted Spicy Nuts *84*, 85

tofu
    Fresh Thai Spring Rolls *34*, 35
    frying 16

tomatoes
    Cocktail Pasties with Tomato
        Sauce *38*, 39
    Corn Cups with Tomato-Corn
        Salsa *46–47*, 64
    peeling and seeding 17
    Roasted Tomato Hearts *38*, 50

tortilla chips 16–17

Tostaditas, Chicken, Chili and
    Avocado *46–47*, 65

vegetables. *See also individual
    vegetables*
    about 11
    Crudités with Lemon-Dill
        Vinaigrette *74*, 75
    Vegetable Bruschetta 51, *51*

vinegars 9

Wild Mushroom Filo Packets *30*, 31

zest 16